SEC 482 CRPC 528 BNSS QUASHING MATTERS- SUPREME COURT'S LATEST CASE LAWS

CASE NOTES- FACTS- FINDINGS OF APEX COURT JUDGES & CITATIONS

JAYPRAKASH BANSILAL SOMANI

Made with ♥ on the Notion Press Platform
www.notionpress.com

Dedicated

To

All the Past & Present Judges of the Supreme Court of India.

Salute to their wisdom.

Salute to their interpretation of Law.

Salute to their elaborative judgement writing.

SUPREME COURT OF INDIA

• • •

Contents

Contents

Preface

Dear Learned Advocates of Trial Court, High court and Supreme Court, Corporate and Individuals.

I am very delighted to provide you a book on SEC 482 CrPC/ 528 BNSS QUASHING MATTERS- SUPREME COURT'S LATEST CASE LAWS.

In this book you will get...

1. Name of the Case i. e. Cause title

2. Relevant Sections discussed in the case

3. Hon'ble Judges/Coram of the case

4.Number of PDF Pages in Original Judgement of the case

5. All available Citations of the case

6. Case Note with appeal allowed/ dismissed or disposed off

7. Facts of the case

8. Hon'ble Apex Court's findings, while dismissing/allowing or disposing the appeal

9. Ratio Decidendi if any.

My special thanks to Manupatra, because of their web portal I can compile this book in well manner. I am also thankful to Notion Press to support me to publish & market this book throughout the Country. Thanks to my Juniors, Advocate Colleagues & Insolvency Professional Colleagues to support me in this venture.

Adv. Manoj Kumar Chowdhary & Adv. Shruti Kriti has helped me a lot to compile this book. I hope this book will add some value addition in the wealth of your legal knowledge. Your positive feedbacks will boost me to compile/ write further books & negative feedbacks will improve my skills. Kindly send your valuable feedbacks by email.

Thanks with Regards,

Jayprakash B. Somani

Advocate, Supreme Court of India

Email: jaysomani64@gmail.com

Web Site:www.jayprakashsomani.com

Call: 9322188701, 8459194576

• • •

Acknowledgements

Printed & Published by
Notion Press
No. 8, 3rd Cross Street,
CIT Colony, Mylapore,
Chennai, Tamil Nadu- 600004

• • •

Managed by
Jayprakash Somani Advocates & Solicitors
Law Firm for Supreme Court of India
Delhi Office
B- 851, 1st Floor, Shivaji Marg, New Ashok Nagar, Delhi 110096.
Call: 9322188701, 8459194576
Supreme Court Chamber
312, 3rd Floor, M. C. Setalvad Block, In front of 'D' Gate, Bhagwan Das
Road, Supreme Court of India, New Delhi 110001
Contact: 8459194576, 9811011747
www.jayprakashsomani.com

• • •

Download our app to get access to our Free Videos, Free Bare Acts, Free
Study Material in Legal as well as International Business Regime.
Android App Link ;-https://clpandrea.page.link/cmSm
Ios APp Link :-https://apps.apple.com/us/app/classplus/id1324522260
Login with org code ;- (qywzji)
Web Link ;-https://qywzji.courses.store/
Opportunity for Lawyers/ Social Workers to get Supreme Court Law
Firm JSAS's authorised centre at District Level.
Kindly Message or Call to: 9322188701

• • •

Books are available online in India
1. **Notion Press:**https://notionpress.com/author/jayprakash_somani
2. **Amazon:**https://www.amazon.in/s?k=jayprakash+somani
3. **Flipkart:**https://www.flipkart.com/search?q=Jayprakash%20Somani

Books are available online at International Market
4. Amazon International: https://www.amazon.com/s?k=jayprakash+somani

5. Amazon United Kingdom: https://www.amazon.co.uk/s?k=jayprakash+somani

6. E-Books/Kindle edition at National & International Level: https://www.amazon.in/s?k=jaypraksh+somani

• • •

CHAPTER I

Supriya Jain vs. State of Haryana and Ors. (04.07.2023 – SC) : MANU/SC/0730/2023

Relative Section:

Code of Criminal Procedure, 1973 (CrPC) - Section 161, Code of Criminal Procedure, 1973 (CrPC) - Section 162, Code of Criminal Procedure, 1973 (CrPC) - Section 173(2), Code of Criminal Procedure, 1973 (CrPC) - Section 228, Code of Criminal Procedure, 1973 (CrPC) - Section 397, Code of Criminal Procedure, 1973 (CrPC) - Section 482; Indian Evidence Act, 1872 - Section 65B; Indian Penal Code, 1860 (IPC) - Section 120B, Section 180, Section 379,Section 406, Section 420, Section 506

Hon'ble Judges/Coram:

S. Ravindra Bhat and Dipankar Datta, JJ.

Equivalent Citation: AIR2023SC3287, 2023/INSC/595, 2023(3)RCR(Criminal)506

Number of Pages in the Original Judgment:8

Case Reference:

Amit Kapoor v. Ramesh Chander and Ors. MANU/SC/0746/2012

Case Note:

Criminal - Proceedings - Power of quashing - Section 482 of Code of Criminal Procedure, 1973 (CrPC) - High Court dismissed the petition under Section 482 of CrPC, hence present appeal - Whether trial against Petitioner ought to be permitted to proceed?

Facts:

Based on a complaint lodged by the second Respondent, was registered under Sections 406, 420, 506 and 120B, Indian Penal Code ("IPC") against 7 Accused which, included the Petitioner The High Court's jurisdiction under Section 482 of CrPC was invoked by the Petitioner subjecting the charge-sheet dated 14th February, 2022, the order of the CJM framing charges dated 18th July, 2022 and the revisional order of the ASJ 27th September, 2022 to challenge. The High Court referred to various judicial precedents outlining the contours of exercise of jurisdiction by the high courts while they are approached for quashing an FIR/a complaint and/or criminal proceedings. Relying on such precedents and based on formation of opinion that there was sufficient material found against the Petitioner in course of investigation, the High Court by its impugned judgment and order spurned the challenge and declined interference resulting in dismissal of the proceedings initiated by the Petitioner. Aggrieved thereby, the unsuccessful Petitioner before the High Court is in appeal.

Held, while dismissing the appeal

1. The charge-sheet contains a list of 27 (twenty-seven) witnesses who are proposed to be examined by the prosecution in support of the charges framed against several Accused including the Petitioner. Apart from the second Respondent and others this particular list includes Indu, the sister-in-law of the second Respondent, who is said to have been present at House No. 620 when allegedly the money changed hands. [16]

2. This is a case where the charges have been framed and the Accused are awaiting trial. Having regard to the totality of the facts and circumstances, present Court is of the considered opinion that the investigation and the follow-up steps are not so patently and unobtrusively defective or erroneous (except to the extent we propose to mention before concluding our judgment) that allowing the trial to progress might cause a miscarriage of justice. This is also not an appropriate stage to delve deep into the records. It is no part of the business of any of the courts to ascertain what the outcome of the trial could be, conviction or acquittal of the Accused. The small window that the law, through judicial precedents, provides is to look at the allegations in the FIR and the materials collected in course of investigation, without a rebuttal thereof by the Accused, and to form an opinion upon consideration thereof that an offence is indeed not disclosed from it. Unless the prosecution is shown to be illegitimate so as to result in an abuse of the process of law, it would not be proper to scuttle it. In Amit Kapoor v. Ramesh Chandra, this Court laid down that, though there are no limits of the powers of the Court Under Section 482 of the CrPC but the more the power, the more due care and caution is to be exercised in invoking these powers. The power of quashing criminal proceedings, particularly, the charge framed in terms of Section 228 of the CrPC should be exercised very sparingly and with circumspection and that too in the rarest of rare cases. [17]

3. It is not one of those rare cases where the uncontroverted allegations appearing from the materials on record notwithstanding, it can successfully be contended that even no prima facie opinion can be formed pointing to commission of any offence by the Petitioner. It is trite that the conspiracy

to commit an offence is by itself distinct from the offence to do which the conspiracy is entered into and that such an offence, if actually committed, would be the subject-matter of a separate charge. The allegations that the Petitioner was found counting the cash received by the principal Accused from the second Respondent in the presence of a listed witness and that she conspired with her sister, the principal Accused, to cheat and defraud the second Respondent, persuade present Court to record that involvement of the Petitioner, howsoever limited, cannot be ruled out at this stage and, therefore, the trial ought to be permitted to proceed and she obliged to stand trial. [18]

4. The impugned judgment and order of the High Court dismissing the petition under Section 482 of CrPC. [19]

5. Appeal dismissed. [24]

Disposition: In Favour of State.

• • •

CHAPTER II

Ramesh Kumar vs. The State of NCT of Delhi (04.07.2023 – SC) : MANU/SC/0731/2023

Relative Section:

Code of Criminal Procedure,1973(CrPC)-Section 173(2),Section 438,Section 438(1),Section 438(2), Sec.482,

Constitution of India - Article 21;

Indian Penal Code, 1860 (IPC) - Section 34, Section 406, Section 420, Section 467, Section 468,Section 471

Hon'ble Judges/Coram: S. Ravindra Bhat and Dipankar Datta, JJ

Equivalent Citation: AIR2023SC3484, 301(2023)DLT66, 2023/INSC/596, (2023)7SCC461

Number of Pages in the Original Judgment: 11

Case Reference:

Munish Bhasin and Ors. v. State (Govt. of N.C.T. of Delhi) and Ors. MANU/SC/0319/2009; Gurbaksh Singh Sibbia and Ors. v. State of Punjab MANU/SC/0215/1980; Maneka Gandhi v. Union of India (UOI) and Ors. MANU/SC/0133/1978; Sumit Mehta v. State of N.C.T. of Delhi MANU/SC/0935/2013; Dilip Singh v. State of Madhya Pradesh and Ors. MANU/SC/0089/2021; Bimla Tiwari v. State of Bihar MANU/SC/0051/2023

Case Category:

CRIMINAL MATTERS - CRIMINAL MATTERS RELATING TO BAIL/INTERIM BAIL/ANTICIPATORY BAIL AND AGAINST SUSPENSION OF SENTENCE

Case Note:

Criminal - Bail - Condition thereto - Section 438 of the Code of Criminal Procedure, 1973 (CrPC) - Issue in present case is with regard to condition for deposit/payment as a pre-requisite for grant of bail - Whether High Court fell in grave error in proceeding on the basis of the undertaking of the Appellant and imposing payment of Rs. 22,00,000 as a condition precedent for grant of bail

Facts:

Appellant approached the High Court seeking an order under Section 438 of the CrPC. Similar approach was made by the builder. The High

Court by its common order dated 24th November, 2022 granted bail to the Appellant and the builder, subject to certain conditions. Expressing his difficulty in arranging for funds to deposit Rs. 22,00,000, the Appellant had applied before the High Court Under Section 482 of the CrPC seeking extension of time to make the requisite deposit. By an order, the said application was disposed of by the High Court granting extension of time by three days, failing which it was directed that anticipatory bail granted to the Appellant shall automatically stand revoked. The Appellant is aggrieved by the aforesaid condition of the impugned judgment and order imposed by the High Court and is now before present Court

Held, while disposing of the appeal

1. Law regarding exercise of discretion while granting a prayer for bail Under Section 438 of the CrPC having been authoritatively laid down by this Court. Assuming that there is substance in the allegation of the complainants that the Appellant (either in connivance with the builder or even in the absence of any such connivance) has cheated the complainants, the investigation is yet to result in a charge-sheet being filed Under Section 173(2) of the Code of Criminal Procedure, not to speak of the alleged offence being proved before the competent trial court in accordance with the settled procedures and the applicable laws. Sub-section (2) of Section 438 of the CrPC does empower the high court or the court of sessions to impose such conditions while making a direction Under Sub-section (1) as it may think fit in the light of the facts of the particular case and such direction may include the conditions as in Clauses (i) to (iv) thereof. However, the conditions to be imposed must not be onerous or unreasonable or excessive. In the context of grant of bail, all such conditions that would facilitate the appearance of the Accused before the investigating officer/court, unhindered completion of investigation/trial and safety of the community assume relevance. However, inclusion of a condition for payment of money by the applicant for bail tends to create an impression that bail could be secured by depositing money alleged to have been cheated. That is really not the purpose and intent of the provisions for grant of bail. In exceptional cases such as where an allegation of misappropriation of public money by the Accused is levelled and the Accused while seeking indulgence of the court to have his liberty secured/restored volunteers to account for the whole or any part of the public money allegedly misappropriated by him, it would be open to the concerned court to consider whether in the larger public interest the money misappropriated

should be allowed to be deposited before the application for anticipatory bail/bail is taken up for final consideration. [26]

2. The version in the FIR, even if taken on face value, discloses payment through cheques of Rs. 17,00,000 in the name of the Appellant and not Rs. 22,00,000. Present Court have not been able to comprehend how the High Court arrived at the latter figure as payable by the Appellant and why the Appellant's counsel as well agreed with such figure. Prima facie, there appears to be some sort of a calculation error. Also, prima facie, there remains some doubt as regards the conduct of the Appellant in receiving cheques from the complainants without there being any agreement inter se. [27]

3. It also does not appear from the materials on record that the complainants have instituted any civil suit for recovery of money allegedly paid by them to the Appellant. If at all the offence alleged against the Appellant is proved resulting in his conviction, he would be bound to suffer penal consequence(s) but despite such conviction he may not be under any obligation to repay the amount allegedly received from the complainants. This too is an aspect which the High Court exercising jurisdiction Under Section 438 of the Code of Criminal Procedure did not bear in mind. [28]

4. High Court fell in grave error in proceeding on the basis of the undertaking of the Appellant and imposing payment of Rs. 22,00,000 as a condition precedent for grant of bail. [29]

5. The matter remitted back to the High Court. [30]

6. Appeal stands disposed of. [34]

Ratio Decidendi: Conditions to be imposed for bail must not be onerous or unreasonable or excessive

Disposition: Disposed of.

• • •

CHAPTER III

Chanchalpati Das vs. The State of West Bengal and Ors. (18.05.2023 – SC) : MANU/SC/0592/2023

Relative Section:

Code of Criminal Procedure, 1973 (CrPC) - Section 155(2), Code of Criminal Procedure, 1973 (CrPC) - Section 156(1), Code of Criminal Procedure, 1973 (CrPC) - Section 156(3), Code of Criminal Procedure, 1973 (CrPC) - Section 320, Code of Criminal Procedure, 1973 (CrPC) - Section 482; Constitution of India - Article 226; Indian Penal Code,1860-Section 120B, Section 379, Section 406, Section 408,Section 411,Section 468, Sec.471

Hon'ble Judges/Coram:

Ajay Rastogi and Bela M. Trivedi, JJ.

Equivalent Citation: AIR2023SC2710, 2023 (2) ALT (Crl.) 245 (A.P.), 2023/INSC/554

Number of Pages in the Original Judgment: 9

Case Reference:

State of Haryana and Ors. v. Ch. Bhajan Lal and Ors. MANU/SC/0115/1992; G. Sagar Suri and Ors. v. State of U.P. and Ors. MANU/SC/0045/2000; Madhavrao Jiwajirao Scindia and Ors. v. Sambhajirao Chandrojirao Angre and Ors. MANU/SC/0261/1988; Subal Ghorai and Ors. v. State of West Bengal MANU/SC/0296/2013; Central Bureau of Investigation v. Maninder Singh MANU/SC/0936/2015; State of Gujarat v. Gajanand M. Dalwadi (D) by Lrs. MANU/SC/8208/2007; Jasbir Singh v. Tara Singh and Ors. MANU/SC/1045/2015; Jagdish Ram v. State of Rajasthan and Ors. MANU/SC/0196/2004; Central Bureau of Investigation v. Arvind Khanna MANU/SC/1432/2019; State of Karnataka v. L. Muniswamy and Ors. MANU/SC/0143/1977; State of Andhra Pradesh v. Golconda Linga Swamy and Ors. MANU/SC/0552/2004; Dalip Singh v. State of U.P. and Ors. MANU/SC/1886/2009; Subrata Roy Sahara v. Union of India (UOI) and Ors. MANU/SC/0406/2014; Hasmukhlal D. Vora and Anr. v. State of Tamil Nadu MANU/SC/1639/2022

Case Note:

Criminal - Quashing of chargesheet - Sections 468, 471, 406 and 120-B of Indian Penal Code, 1860 (IPC); Section 482 of Code of Criminal Procedure, 1973 (CrPC) - Appeals arise out of the common judgment passed by the High Court whereby the High Court has dismissed both the Applications seeking quashing of the charge-sheet filed against the Appellants-Accused, in respect of the FIR registered for the offences Under Sections 468, 471, 406 and 120-B of IPC - Whether criminal proceedings pending against the Appellants are liable to be quashed?

Facts:

The Appellants filed a petition before the High Court seeking quashing of proceedings of criminal case pending before the CJM, Alipore. The High Court vide the common impugned judgement and order dismissed both the Criminal Revisions. The Appellants vehemently submitted that the prosecution initiated against the Appellants by the Respondent-complainant was only an attempt to harass the Appellants under the guise of the bus theft case to settle the personal scores with Appellants. He further submitted that the allegations in the complaint/FIR are not only absurd and improbable, but there is no reasonable possibility of the Appellants being convicted for the alleged offences after the trial.

Held, while allowing the appeal

1. Even as per the case of the complainant, the alleged incident of bus theft had taken place in the year 2001, and it was only in 2009 that the substantial complaint was made in the Court of Chief Judicial Magistrate, Alipore. It is just not believable that the concerned Ballygunge Police Station, Kolkata would not have taken any action on the report made in 2002 on behalf of the powerful body like the ISKCON Kolkata, or on the letter dated 30.09.2006 written by the Branch Manager of the ISKCON, Kolkata. The Respondent No. 2- complainant also did not take any concrete action for getting the said complaint registered with regard to the alleged theft of bus for a long period of eight years, till the complaint in the Court was filed in the year 2009. In the opinion of the Court such an inordinate delay of eight years in filing the complaint in the court itself would be a sufficient ground to quash the proceedings. If the luxury bus owned by the ISKCON, Kolkata Branch in 1998 was so precious to them, they would not have sat silent for such a long time of eight years. The criminal machinery set into motion by filing the complaint for the alleged incident which had taken place eight years ago, that act itself was nothing but a sheer misuse and abuse of the process of the court. [11]

2. Except bald allegations made in the complaint with regard to the theft of bus in question there was no material or document produced by the complainant to substantiate the allegations against the Appellants. Even after the investigation of the said complaint, there was no evidence collected by the investigating officer to prima facie satisfy the ingredients constituting the alleged offences under Sections 468, 471, 406 and 120B of IPC. Even if the allegations made in the complaint as well as in the Chargesheet are taken at their face value none of the ingredients constituting the alleged offences are culled out. There was no expert opinion obtained or scientific evidence collected on the documents allegedly forged to show as to by whom, when and how the theft of vehicle and forgery of documents were committed. Under the circumstances, allowing such prosecution to continue would not only be an empty formality but would be gross wastage of court's precious time. [12]

3. High Courts have power to quash the proceedings in exercise of powers Under Section 482 of CrPC to prevent the abuse of process of any Court or otherwise to secure the ends of justice. Though the powers Under Section 482 should be sparingly exercised and with great caution, the said powers ought to be exercised if a clear case of abuse of process of law is made out by the Accused. [13]

4. The complaint filed by the Respondent-complainant after an inordinate unexplained delay of eight years was nothing but sheer misuse and abuse of the process of law to settle the personal scores with the Appellants, and that continuation of such malicious prosecution would also be further abuse and misuse of process of law, more particularly when neither the allegations made in the complaint nor in the chargesheet, disclose any prima facie case against the Appellants. The allegations made against the Appellants are so absurd and improbable that no prudent person can ever reach to a conclusion that there is a sufficient ground for proceeding against the Appellants-Accused. [17]

5. Present Court deem it appropriate to quash the criminal proceedings pending against the Appellants in the Court of Chief Judicial Magistrate, Alipore, arising out of the FIR registered at Ballygunge Police Station, and quash the same. [21]

6. Appeals allowed. [22]

Ratio Decidendi: Though the powers under Section 482 of CrPC should be sparingly exercised, the said powers ought to be exercised if a clear case of abuse of process of law is made out by the Accused

Disposition: In Favour of Accused.

• • •

Y. Balaji vs. Karthik Desari and Ors. (16.05.2023 – SC) : MANU/SC/0584/2023

Relative Section:

Arms Act 1959 - Section 25; Code of Criminal Procedure, 1973 (CrPC) - Section 160, Section 161, Section 164, Section 173, Section 173(2), Section 173(8), Section 216, - Section 482;

Constitution of India - Article 20(3), Article 21, Article 22;

Indian Evidence Act, 1872 - Section 65B;

Indian Penal Code, 1860 (IPC) - Section 34, Section 109, Section 120B, Section 201,Section 302,Section 406, Section 419, Section 420, Section 465, Section 467,Section 471,Section 506(1);

Prevention Of Corruption Act, 1988 - Section 7, Section 12, Section 13,Section 13(1), Section 13(2);

Prevention Of Money-laundering Act, 2002 - Section 2(1), Section 3, Section 3(2), Section 8, Section 50, Section 50(2), Section 63, Section 66(2)

Hon'ble Judges/Coram:

Krishna Murari and V. Ramasubramanian, JJ.

Equivalent Citation: AIR2023SC3171, 2023/INSC/542, 2023(3)MLJ(Crl)113, 2023 (2) MWN (CR.) 679

Number of Pages in the Original Judgment: 42

Case Reference:

Vinay Tyagi v. Irshad Ali and Ors. MANU/SC/1101/2012; Union of India v. Ganpati Dealcom Private Limited MANU/SC/1028/2022; Central Board of Dawoodi Bohra Community v. State of Maharashtra MANU/SC/ 0120/2023; Janata Dal v. H.S. Chowdhary and Ors. MANU/SC/0532/1992; Simranjit Singh Mann v. Union of India (UOI) and Ors. MANU/SC/0058/ 1993; Bihta Co-operative Development Cane Marketing Union Ltd. and Ors. v. The Bank of Bihar and Ors. MANU/SC/0260/1966; Shauqin Singh and Ors. v. Desa Singh and Ors. MANU/SC/0388/1969; Kantaru Rajeevaru* v. Indian Young Lawyers Association and Ors. MANU/SC/0443/2020; Asgar Ali v. The State of Jammu and Kashmir and Ors. MANU/SC/1116/2021; Badrinath v. Government of Tamil Nadu and Ors. MANU/SC/0624/2000; State of Punjab v. Davinder Pal Singh Bhullar and Ors. MANU/SC/1476/

2011; Management of Northern Railway Co-operative Society Ltd. v. Industrial Tribunal, Rajasthan, Jaipur and Ors. MANU/SC/0221/1967; P. Dharamaraj v. Shanmugam MANU/SC/1119/2022; Sakshi and Ors. v. Union of India (UOI) and Ors. MANU/SC/0523/2004; Enforcement Directorate v. Gagandeep Singh MANU/DE/0535/2022; Vijay Madanlal Choudhary v. Union of India MANU/SC/0924/2022; Central Board of Dawoodi Bohra Community and Ors. v. State of Maharashtra and Ors. MANU/SC/1069/2004

Case Note:

Criminal -De novo investigation -Quashing of summons - Sections 34, 406 and 420 of Indian Penal Code, 1860, Sections 2(1)(u) and 3 of Prevention of Money-Laundering Act, 2002, Section 173(8) of Code of Criminal Procedure, 1973 and Section 65B of Indian Evidence Act, 1872- High Court ordered de novo investigation in petition filed at instance of complainant alleging that accused person received money for securing job of Conductor for his son and thereby committed offence punishable under Sections 406 and 420 read with Section 34 of Code - Thereafter, writ petitions filed before High Court challenging summons issued by ED - High Court quashed summons on ground that one of four calendar cases had already been quashed by High Court on basis of Joint Compromise Memo - High Court further refused to extend time for completion of investigation - Hence, present appeals - Whether High Court erred in ordering de novo investigation in alleged offence, quashing summons issued by ED and in refusing to extend time for completion of investigation.

Facts:

The High Court passed an order allowing the petition filed by complainant and ordered a de novo investigation in petition filed alleging that accused person received a sumfor securing the job of a Conductor for his son and that he and his accomplices committed offences punishable under Sections 406 and 420 read with Section 34 Indian Penal Code. Thereafter, three writ petitions came to be filed, by accused persons challenging the summons issued by ED. These writ petitions were allowed by the High Court by an order primarily on the ground that one of the four calendar cases had already been quashed by the High Court on the basis of a Joint Compromise Memo and that further proceedings in the other calendar cases had been stayed by the High Court. The High Court further refused to extend the time for completion of investigation.

Held, while disposing off the appeals:

(i) Though the original petition and the arguments recorded in the impugned order did not reflect one particular ground, the operative portion of the impugned order allows de novo investigation on a ground not raised in the petition. In the impugned order, it was recorded by the High Court that as per the affidavit filed by the Investigating Officer, the investigating agency had seized the register used for entering interview marks and sent the same to the Forensic Department for analysis to find out the manipulations and that the Final Report under Section 173(8) of the Code was filed even before the receipt of the report of the Forensic Department. It was on this contention that the High Court thought fit to order de novo investigation not only in the case in which complainant sought de novo investigation but also in all the criminal cases. What was interesting was that the order directing de novo investigation in all the three cases, had actually inured to the benefit of the Accused, but the High Court put it on the ground that the credibility of the investigation should not be eroded. In fact, the Accused did not seek de novo investigation on the ground of slackness on the part of the Investigating Officer, but it was complainant who sought it, with the able assistance of the Investigating Officer.[19]

(ii) By issuing the direction, the High Court not only directed the wiping out of the investigation carried out so far, but virtually wiped out even the judgment of this Court passed in Criminal Appeal.[22]

(iii) The High Court had not quashed the summons issued by ED. The High Court had merely injuncted ED from proceeding further till the clog on the cases relating to the predicate offences was removed.[67]

(iv) Even if an intangible property was derived as a result of criminal activity relating to a scheduled offence, it becomes proceeds of crime under Section 2(1)(u). This court was not impressed with the contention that the investigation by ED was triggered without any foundational/jurisdictional facts. In our view, the allegations in the FIR point out to involvement of persons in criminal activity relating to scheduled offences, the generation as well as laundering of the proceeds of crime within the meaning of Section 3. This was in view of the fact that wherever there are allegations of corruption, there was acquisition of proceeds of crime which itself tantamount to money-laundering.[104]

(v) Section 65B concerns the admissibility of electronic records. Without certification, ED may not be able to use those electronic records in evidence, in the prosecution under PMLA. But it did not mean that they could not even have a look at the electronic record.[123]

(vi) When a petition for extension of time was moved, the Court rejected on the ground that the prayer had become infructuous. Therefore, worried about the fate of further investigation, the victim had come up with the appeal. But the worry of the Appellant is baseless. Merely because the High Court had not granted extension of time, it does not mean that the direction to conduct further investigation had become infructuous. On the contrary, a Final Report had already been filed under Section 173(8) of the Code.[125]

• • •

CHAPTER V

Gulam Mustafa vs. The State of Karnataka and Ors. (10.05.2023 – SC) : MANU/SC/0556/2023

Relative Section:

Code of Criminal Procedure, 1973 (CrPC) - Section 155(2), Code of Criminal Procedure, 1973 (CrPC) - Section 156(1), Code of Criminal Procedure, 1973 (CrPC) - Section 482; Constitution of India - Article 15, Constitution of India - Article 17, Constitution of India - Article 21, Constitution of India - Article 142, Constitution of India - Article 226; Indian Penal Code, 1860 (IPC) - Section 34, Indian Penal Code, 1860 (IPC) - Section 120B, Indian Penal Code, 1860 (IPC) - Section 406, Indian Penal Code, 1860 (IPC) - Section 419, Indian Penal Code, 1860 (IPC) - Section 420, Indian Penal Code, 1860 (IPC) - Section 427, Indian Penal Code, 1860 (IPC) - Section 448, Indian Penal Code, 1860 (IPC) - Section 468, Indian Penal Code, 1860 (IPC) - Section 471; Scheduled Castes And The Scheduled Tribes (prevention Of Atrocities) Act, 1989 - Section 3(1)

Hon'ble Judges/Coram:

Dinesh Maheshwari and Ahsanuddin Amanullah, JJ.

Equivalent Citation: AIR2023SC2999, 2023/INSC/511, 2023(4)KarLJ561, 2023(3)RCR(Criminal)182

Number of Pages in the Original Judgment:11

Case Reference:

Govind Prasad Kejriwal v. State of Bihar and Ors. MANU/SC/0112/2020; The Commissioner of Police and Ors. v. Devender Anand and Ors. MANU/SC/1058/2019; Binod Kumar v. State of Bihar MANU/SC/0978/2014; Indian Oil Corporation v. NEPC India Ltd. and Ors. MANU/SC/3152/2006; G. Sagar Suri and Ors. v. State of U.P. and Ors. MANU/SC/0045/2000; State of Madhya Pradesh v. Surendra Kori MANU/SC/0832/2012; Dineshbhai Chandubhai Patel and Ors. v. State of Gujarat and Ors. MANU/SC/0004/2018; Satvinder Kaur v. State (Govt. of N.C.T. of Delhi) and Ors. MANU/SC/0632/1999; P. Chidambaram v. Directorate of Enforcement MANU/SC/1209/2019; Skoda Auto Volkswagen India Private Limited v. The State of Uttar Pradesh and Ors. MANU/SC/0898/2020; Union of India (UOI) v. Prakash P. Hinduja and Ors. MANU/SC/0446/2003;

Superintendent of Police, C.B.I. and Ors. v. Tapan Kr. Singh MANU/SC/0299/2003; State of U.P. v. Naresh and Ors. MANU/SC/0228/2011; State of Haryana and Ors. v. Ch. Bhajan Lal and Ors. MANU/SC/0115/1992; State of Karnataka v. M. Devendrappa and Ors. MANU/SC/0027/2002; Uma Shankar Gopalika v. State of Bihar and Ors. MANU/SC/1233/2004; Parbatbhai Aahir and Ors. v. State of Gujarat and Ors. MANU/SC/1241/2017; The State of Telangana v. Habib Abdullah Jeelani and Ors. MANU/SC/0020/2017; Vinod Natesan v. State of Kerala and Ors. MANU/SC/1470/2018; Kamal Shivaji Pokarnekar v. The State of Maharashtra and Ors. MANU/SC/0180/2019; Mahendra K.C. v. The State of Karnataka and Ors. MANU/SC/1012/2021; Arnab Manoranjan Goswami v. The State of Maharashtra and Ors. MANU/SC/0902/2020; Neeharika Infrastructure Pvt. Ltd. v. State of Maharashtra and Ors. MANU/SC/0272/2021; Ramawatar v. State of Madhya Pradesh MANU/SC/0967/2021

Case Note:

Criminal - Civil nature - Quashing of proceedings - Sections 120B, 406, 419, 420, 427, 448, 468 and 471 of Indian Penal Code, 1860 and Section 3(1)(15) of Scheduled Castes and Scheduled Tribes Act, 1989-Appellant was Managing Director of company which was said to be engaged in developing residential properties - Said company and owners entered into Joint Development Agreement - Apartment project, as contemplated under JDA, was completed and sale deeds were executed in favour of allottees - First Information Report was registered against Appellant under Section 3(1)(15) of Act and Sections 427, 420, 419, 406, 471, 468, 448 and 120B of Code - Appellant moved petition before High Court for quashing FIR - However, Criminal Petition was ultimately dismissed -Hence, present appeal - Whether impugned proceedings liable to be quashed.

Facts:

The Appellant was the Managing Director of company. The company was said to be engaged in developing residential properties. The said company and the ownersof land entered into a Joint Development Agreement. The apartment project, as contemplated under the JDA, was completed and sale deeds were executed in favour of the allottees. First Information Report was registered under against appellant under Section 3(11)(15) of Act, 1989 and Sections 427, 420, 419, 406, 471, 468, 448 and 120B of Code. The Appellant moved a petition before the High Court for quashing the FIR. However, Criminal Petition was ultimately dismissed.

Held, while allowing the appeal:

(i) This Court had been consistent in interfering in such matters where purely civil disputes, more often than not, relating to land and/or money are given the colour of criminality, only for the purposes of exerting extra-judicial pressure on the party concerned, which,is nothing but abuse of the process of the court. In the present case, there was a huge, and quite frankly, unexplained delay of over sixty years in initiating dispute with regard to the ownership of the land in question, and the criminal case has been lodged only after failure to obtain relief in the civil suits, coupled with denial of relief in the interim therein to the Respondent No. 2/her family members. It was evident that resort was now being had to criminal proceedings which, in the considered opinion of this Court, was with ulterior motives, for oblique reasons and was a clear case of vengeance. [36]

(ii) The Court would also note that even if the allegations are taken to be true on their face value, it was not discernible that any offence could be said to have been made out under the SC/ST Act against the Appellant. The complaint and FIR were frivolous, vexatious and oppressive. [37]

(iii) This Court would indicate that the officers, who institute an FIR, based on any complaint, were duty-bound to be vigilant before invoking any provision of a very stringent statute, like the SC/ST Act, which imposes serious penal consequences on the concerned Accused. The officer had to be satisfied that the provisions he seeks to invoke prima facie apply to the case at hand. The remarks of this court, in no manner, were to dilute the applicability of special/stringent statues, but only to remind the police not to mechanically apply the law, dehors reference to the factual position. [38]

Disposition: In Favour of Accused.

• • •

CHAPTER VI

Priyanka Mishra and Ors. vs. The State of Madhya Pradesh and Ors. (08.05.2023 – SC) : MANU/SC/0620/2023

Relative Section:

Code of Criminal Procedure, 1973 (CrPC) - Section 161, Code of Criminal Procedure, 1973 (CrPC) - Section 164, Code of Criminal Procedure, 1973 (CrPC) - Section 482; Dowry Prohibition Act, 1961 - Section 4; Indian Penal Code, 1860 (IPC) - Section 34, Indian Penal Code, 1860 (IPC) - Section 498A

Hon'ble Judges/Coram:

Sanjay Kishan Kaul and Ahsanuddin Amanullah, JJ.

Equivalent Citation: 2023(2)JLJ486, 2023(3)RCR(Criminal)91

Number of Pages in the Original Judgment: 6

Case Reference:

Rajesh Sharma and Ors. v. State of U.P. and Ors. MANU/SC/0909/2017; State of Haryana and Ors. v. Ch. Bhajan Lal and Ors. MANU/SC/0115/1992; Pawan Kumar and Ors. v. State of Haryana MANU/SC/0104/1998; Mahendra K.C. v. The State of Karnataka and Ors. MANU/SC/1012/2021; Central Bureau of Investigation v. A. Ravishankar Prasad and Ors. MANU/SC/0808/2009; S. Mahaboob Basha v. The State of Karnataka MANU/SC/0908/2014; Rupali Devi v. State of Uttar Pradesh and Ors. MANU/SC/0499/2019; Kahkashan Kausar alias Sonam v. State of Bihar, MANU/SC/0163/2022

Case Note:

Criminal -Quashing of FIR - Section 482 of the Code of Criminal Procedure, 1973 (CrPC) - Present Appeal is directed against the Final judgment passed by the High Court by which the petition filed by the Appellants Under Section 482 of the Code of Criminal Procedure, 1973 (CrPC) praying to quash First Information Report registered at P.S. has been dismissed - Whether FIR registered at Police Station is liable to be quashed?

Facts:

The Appellants are the sister-in-law, mother-in-law and father-in-law of the Respondent No. 2. As per the complaint filed by Respondent No.

2 before the police, the Appellants and the husband of the Respondent No. 2 were made Accused for offences punishable Under Section 498-A and Section 34 of the Indian Penal Code, 1860 ("IPC") and Section 4 of the Dowry Prohibition Act. Present Appeal is directed against the Final judgment passed by the High Court by which the petition filed by the Appellants under Section 482 of the CrPC praying to quash First Information Report registered at P.S. has been dismissed

Held, while allowing the appeal

1. FIR in question, as far as the Appellants are concerned, is an abuse of the process of the court. From a plain but careful reading of the material brought on record, including the statements of Respondent No. 2 under Sections 161 and 164 of the CrPC and also of other witnesses, the allegations insofar as they relate to the Appellants seem far-fetched and do not inspire confidence. The facts in totality evince that Respondent No. 2 resided for less than three weeks in the matrimonial home from the date the marriage was solemnised, then lived with her husband at Hyderabad for quite some time and, finally moved to London and then Sweden. Subsequently, Respondent No. 2 upon returning to India, filed the criminal case in question. The same is a retaliatory tactic, inasmuch as the Appellants herein are concerned. [21]

2. Once in Sweden, where the Respondent No. 2 was living with her husband, a divorce petition had been filed, there was no occasion per se, for Respondent No. 2 after coming from Sweden to visit the matrimonial home, much less reside there. [22]

3. Moreover, the husband of Respondent No. 2 having e- mailed a complaint, 3 days prior to the wife lodging her complaint, to the Superintendent of Police, Gwalior, with regard to threat having been received from Respondent No. 2 to implicate the husband and his family members, is clearly indicative that the charges, at least, as against the instant Appellants are an afterthought. [23]

4. The Appellants are to be protected against vexatious and unwarranted criminal prosecution, and from unnecessarily being put through the rigours of an eventual trial. [25]

5. Impugned judgment is set aside. FIR registered at Police Station stands quashed qua the Appellants. Appeal allowed. [26]

Disposition: In Favour of Accused.

• • •

CHAPTER VII

Kailash Vijayvargiya vs. Rajlakshmi Chaudhuri and Ors. (04.05.2023 – SC) : MANU/SC/0527/2023

Relative Section:

Code of Criminal Procedure, 1973 (CrPC) - Section 2(d),Section 41,Section 41(1),Section 154, Section 154(1), Section 154(3), Section 155(2), Section 156, Section 156(1), Section 156(2), Section 156(3), Section 157,Section 157(1), Section 159, Section 160, Section 161, Section 162,Section 163,Section 164, Section 165, Section 173, Section 173(1A), Section 173(3), Section 176, Section 190 to ,Section 210, Section 468, Sec. 482;

Constitution of India - Article 21, Constitution of India - Article 226;

Indian Penal Code, 1860 (IPC) - Section 34, Section 120B, Section 166A, Section 313, Section 323,Section 325,Section 341, Section 376, Section 406, Section 417, Section 506, Section 506(ii);

Securitisation& Reconstruction Of Financial Assets And Enforcement Of Security Interest Act, 2002 – Sec. 32

Hon'ble Judges/Coram: M.R. Shah and Sanjiv Khanna, JJ.

Equivalent Citation: 2023 (2) ALT (Crl.) 187 (A.P.), 2023(2)Crimes384(SC), 2023/INSC/494, 2023(2) J.L.J.R.349, 2023(2)KLJ897, 2023(3)KLT431, 2023 (2) MWN (CR.) 18, 2023(2)PLJR359

Number of Pages in the Original Judgment: 24

Case Reference:

Lalita Kumari v. Govt. of U.P. and Ors. MANU/SC/1166/2013; Priyanka Srivastava and Ors. v. State of U.P. and Ors. MANU/SC/0344/2015; Mukul Roy v. State of West Bengal and Ors. MANU/WB/1121/2018; Maksud Saiyed v. State of Gujarat and Ors. MANU/SC/7923/2007; Anil Kumar and Ors. v. M.K. Aiyappa and Ors. MANU/SC/1002/2013; Ramdev Food Products Private Limited v. State of Gujarat MANU/SC/0286/2015; Srinivas Gundluri and Ors. v. SEPCO Electric Power Construction Corporation and Ors. MANU/SC/0539/2010; Anju Chaudhary v. State of U.P. and Ors. MANU/SC/1129/2012; Assistant Collector of Customs and Ors. v. L.R. Malwani and Ors. MANU/SC/0279/1968; Krishna Lal Chawla and Ors. v. State of U.P. and Ors. MANU/SC/0161/2021; Abhinandan Jha and Ors. v. Dinesh Mishra MANU/SC/0054/1967; State of Haryana and Ors. v. Ch. Bhajan Lal and Ors. MANU/SC/0115/1992; HDFC Securities Ltd. and Ors. v. State of Maharashtra and Ors. MANU/SC/1573/2016; Chandra Deo Singh v. Prokash Chandra Bose and Ors. MANU/SC/0053/1963; Jasraj Inder Singh v. Hemraj Multanchand MANU/SC/0016/1977; Gopal Das Sindhi and Ors. v. The State of Assam and Ors. MANU/SC/0413/1961; Suresh Chand Jain v. State of Madhya Pradesh and Ors. MANU/SC/0014/2001; Mona Panwar v. The Hon'ble High Court of Judicature at Allahabad through its Registrar and Ors. MANU/SC/0087/2011

Case Note:

Criminal -Registration of FIR - Maintainability of - Sections 156, 156(3), 202 and 468 of Code of Criminal Procedure, 1973 - Respondent No. 1-original complainant lodged complaint under Section 156(3) of Code in Court of CJM, making allegations against Appellants alleging that she was raped by all three Appellants at residence of original Accused No. 3 -CJM after giving cogent reasons, dismissed said application under Section 156(3) of Code - Feeling aggrieved and dissatisfied, complainant preferred Revision Application before High Court - High Court had allowed said revision application and had quashed and set aside order passed by CJM, dismissing application under Section 156(3) of Code and remitted matter to judicial magistrate for further examination -Hence, present appeal - Whether High Court had erred in quashing and setting aside order passed by CJM, dismissing application under Section 156(3) of Code for registration of FIR.

Facts:

Respondent No. 1-original complainant lodged a complaint under Section 156(3) of Code of Criminal Procedure in the Court of CJM, making allegations against the Appellants herein alleging that she was raped by all the three Appellantsat the residence of original Accused No. 3. It was prayed to direct the Officer in Charge of Police Station to start investigation into the matter after treating the complaint as an FIR. The CJM, by a detailed order and after giving cogent reasons, dismissed the said application under Section 156(3) Code of Criminal Procedure.Feeling aggrieved and dissatisfied with the order passed by the CJM, dismissing the application under Section 156(3) Code of Criminal Procedure filed by the complainant, the complainant preferred Revision Application before the High Court. By the impugned judgment and order, the High Court had allowed the said revision application and had quashed and set aside order passed by the CJM, dismissing the application under Section 156(3) Code of Criminal Procedure, mainly relying upon the decision of this Court in the case of Lalita Kumari v. Government of Uttar Pradesh and Ors. and holding that as held by this Court in the case of Lalita Kumari, the police authority in case of preliminary inquiry prior to the registration of a case concerning cognizable offence, had no jurisdiction to verify the veracity of the allegations and therefore a Magistrate cannot verify the truth and veracity of the allegations contained in the application under Section 156(3) Code of Criminal Procedure and therefore the CJM acted contrary to the law laid down by this Court in the case of Lalita Kumari, while entering into the truth and veracity of the allegations. It had been further held that the CJM ought not to have dismissed the application under Section 156(3) Code of Criminal Procedure on the ground that there was a delay of two years in lodging the complaint, which aspect can be considered only at the time of trial.

Held, while disposing off the appeal:

(i) This Court in Priyanka Srivastava case referred to the nature of power exercised by the Magistrate under Section 156(3) of the Code and after referring to several earlier judgments held that the direction for registration of an FIR should not be issued in a routine manner. The Magistrate is required to apply his mind and exercise his discretion in a judicious manner. If the Magistrate finds that the allegations made before him disclose commission of a cognizable offence, he can forward the complaint to the Police for investigation under Section 156 and thereby save valuable time of the Magistrate from being wasted in inquiry as it is primarily the duty of the Police to investigate. However, the Magistrate also has the power to take cognizance and take recourse to procedure under Section 202 of the Code and postpone the issue of process where the Magistrate is yet to determine existence of sufficient ground to proceed. In a third category of cases, the Court may not take cognizance or direct registration of an FIR, but direct preliminary inquiry in terms of the dictum in Lalita Kumari's case. [27]

(ii) It was noticeable that the complainant/informant has made several allegations of rape, sexual harassment, etc. against persons with whom she had been acquainted and working. The complainant/ informant had pleaded threat and harassment at the hands of the persons named as perpetrators, who were people of influence and power as the ground and reason for delay. She pleads that period of limitation prescribed in Section 468 of the Code did not apply to an offence punishable with imprisonment exceeding three years. On the question of delay, reliance was placed on the constitutional bench decision of this Court in the L.R. Melwani. It was submitted that this Court on several occasions had sustained conviction relying solely upon the testimony of the prosecution/victim, when there was no doubt about her credibility and trustworthiness. While examining the question of delay in making the complaint, the courts must remain alive to the fact that it was difficult for a woman to come forward and make a statement alleging rape or sexual assault. [34]

(iii) This court did not intend to go into the question of the merits of the allegations, and what procedure the Magistrate should follow as this was an aspect which the Magistrate must first consider and decide judiciously and as per the law. What was impermissible and contrary to law was an adjudication on merits of the allegations and determination of the facts as baseless, without further scrutiny and examination. Therefore, the High Court was correct in remitting the matter to the judicial magistrate for further examination. [37]

Ratio Decidendi: Once an offence is disclosed, an investigation into the offence must necessarily follow in the interest of justice.

Disposition: Disposed of.

• • •

CHAPTER VIII

Peethambaran vs. State of Kerala and Ors. (03.05.2023 – SC) : MANU/SC/0522/2023

Relative Section:

Code of Criminal Procedure, 1973 (CrPC) - Section 155(2), Section 156(1), Section 156(3), Section 173, Section 173(2), Section 173(8), Section 190, Section 482;

Constitution of India - Article 226; Indian Penal Code, 1860 (IPC) - Section 415, Section 420

Hon'ble Judges/Coram: Krishna Murari and Sanjay Karol, JJ.

Equivalent Citation: 2023(2)ACR1793, 2023(246)AIC129, 2023 (124) ACC 325, 2023 (2) ALT (Crl.) 365 (A.P.), 2023(2)Crimes378(SC), 2023(2)CriminalCC406, 2023/INSC/481, 2023(3)J.L.J.R.144, 2023(2)KLJ816, 2023(3)KLT493, 2023(II)OLR1, 2023(3)PLJR24

Number of Pages in the Original Judgment: 9

Case Reference:

Vinay Tyagi v. Irshad Ali and Ors. MANU/SC/1101/2012; T.T. Antony v. State of Kerala and Ors. MANU/SC/0365/2001; Vinubhai Haribhai Malaviya and Ors. v. The State of Gujarat and Ors. MANU/SC/1427/2019; Randhir Singh Rana v. The State Being the Delhi Administration MANU/SC/0161/1997; G.V. Rao v. L.H.V. Prasad and Ors. MANU/SC/3156/2000; Hari Prasad Chamaria v. Bishun Kumar Surekha and Ors. MANU/SC/0112/1973; Minu Kumari and Ors. v. The State of Bihar and Ors. MANU/SC/8098/2006; Hemant Dhasmana v. Central Bureau of Investigation and Ors. MANU/SC/0459/2001; R.K. Vijayasarathy and Ors. v. Sudha Seetharam and Ors. MANU/SC/0213/2019; Neeharika Infrastructure Pvt. Ltd. v. State of Maharashtra MANU/SC/0272/2021; Devendra Nath Singh v. State of Bihar and Ors. MANU/SC/1306/2022; Vijay Kumar Ghai and Ors. v. State of West Bengal and Ors. MANU/SC/0348/2022

Case Note:

Criminal - Further investigation - Quashing of proceeding - Sections 482 of Code of Criminal Procedure, 1973 and Section 420 of Indian Penal Code, 1860 - Appellant had been charged for offence punishable under Section 420 of Code for having cheated, alongside Accused No.1 - FIR was registered and Final Report (FR-I) placed on record records that as there was no proper evidence in this regard, it shall be considered as false case - Interestingly, another Final Report (FR-II) forms part of record states that witness-Inspector of Police, conducted further investigation as per order passed by District Police Chief - High court had not quashed proceedings subject of petition under Section 482 of Code - Hence, present appeal - Whether under recognized parameters of exercise of power under Section 482, in facts of present case, non- exercise of power was justified and District Police Chief could have ordered further investigation pursuant to which second final report was filed.

Facts:

The Appellant had been charged under Section 420 of the Indian Penal Code, 1860, for having cheated, alongside Accused No. 1, now deceased, the de-facto complainant, and seven other persons of a sum in exchange for securing jobs. An FIR was registered and Final report (FR-I) placed on record records that the complainant was asked to produce documents in this regard, but despite notice, the same were not produced, nor were any other documents, in regards to any financial transaction. Interestingly, another Final Report (FR-II) forms part of the record. It states that witness-Inspector of Police, conducted further investigation as per Order passed by the District Police Chief. It had been urged by way of this appeal that in effect, a re- investigation had been ordered, in violation of the procedure laid down in law. The High court had also not quashed the proceedings subject of the petition under Section 482 of Code.

Held, while allowing the appeal:

(i) The Chief Police Officer of a district was the Superintendent of Police who was an officer of the Indian Police Service. An order from the District Police Chief was not the same as an order issued by the concerned Magistrate. Referring to Vinay Tyagi case, this Court in Devendra Nath Singh v. State of Bihar and Ors. noted that there is no specific requirement to seek leave of the court for further investigation or to file a supplementary report but investigation agencies, have not only understood it to be so but have also adopted the same as a legal requirement. The doctrine of contemporaneaexposito aids such an interpretation of matters which have been long understood and implemented in a particular manner to be accepted into the interpretive process. In other words, the requirement of permission for further investigation or to file a supplementary report is accepted within law and is therefore required to be complied with. [19]

(ii) In the facts at hand, it was clear that such a permission was never taken, granted or ordered. Consequently, FR-II was without basis. In FR-I it had been stated that in the absence of any documents in respect of the financial transactions, the instant case may be treated as a false case. This, then would necessarily imply that after due investigation conducted by a duly authorized person, the conclusion was that the ingredients of the Section mentioned in the FIR had not been met and no case was made out. [20]

(iii) Significantly, no material has been placed on record to show that the representation made by Accused No. 1 (now deceased), the present Appellant or the de facto complainant, was false or that they had prior knowledge of such representation being false and made only with the intention to deceive. There were only statements to the effect that despite reminders by the seven persons no jobs were secured for them or their wives. The only ingredient out of the four required, being in the present case was that in the ordinary course, none of the persons would have given the Accused any money, and therefore were induced to deliver property which otherwise they would have not. No proof of any financial transaction was on record, much less concerning the present Appellant. [25]

(iv) With only one ingredient being fulfilled and mere statements made to show dishonest intention or falsity of statement, the threshold of Section 420 was not breached, constituting the offence. [26]

Disposition: In Favour of Accused.

• • •

CHAPTER IX

Shilpa Sailesh vs. Varun Sreenivasan (01.05.2023 – SC) : MANU/SC/0502/2023

Relative Section:

Code of Civil Procedure, 1908 (CPC) - Section 89, Section 151; Section 125, Section 320, Section 321, Section 482;

Constitution of India-Article32,Article136, Article 141, Article 142, Article 142(1), Article 145(3), Article 226;

Family Courts Act, 1984 - Section 9;

Hindu Marriage Act, 1955 - Section 5,Section 9, Section 13, Section 13B, Section 13(1), 13B(1), 13B(2), 23(1), Section 23(2);

Indian Penal Code, 1860 (IPC) - Section 494, Indian Penal Code, 1860 (IPC) - Section 498A

Hon'bleJudges/Coram:

Sanjay Kishan Kaul, Sanjiv Khanna, Abhay Shreeniwas Oka, Vikram Nath and J.K. Maheshwari, JJ.

Equivalent Citation:

2023(4)ABR180, 2023(4)ALD1, 2023(3)ALT36, 2023(3)CTC550, 299(2023)DLT458, II(2023)DMC201SC, 2023 (3) KHC 435, (2023)3MLJ617, 2023 (2) MWN 689, 2023(3)RCR(Civil)107

Number of Pages in the Original Judgment: 30

Case Reference:

Manish Goel v. Rohini Goel MANU/SC/0106/2010; Pradip Chandra Parija and Ors. v. Pramod Chandra Patnaik and Ors. MANU/SC/0304/2002; M. Siddiq (D) thr. L.Rs. v. Mahant Suresh Das and Ors. MANU/SC/1538/2019; I.C. Golak Nath and Ors. v. State of Punjab and Ors. MANU/SC/0029/1967; Union Carbide Corporation and Ors. v. Union of India (UOI) and Ors. MANU/SC/0058/1992; Prem Chand Garg v. Excise Commissioner, U.P., Allahabad MANU/SC/0082/1962; Supreme Court Bar Association v. Union of India (UOI) and Ors. MANU/SC/0291/1998; Amardeep Singh v. Harveen Kaur MANU/SC/1134/2017; Amit Kumar v. Suman Beniwal MANU/SC/1293/2021; B.S. Joshi and Ors. v. State of Haryana and Ors. MANU/SC/0230/2003; Gian Singh v. State of Punjab and Ors. MANU/SC/0781/2012; Jitendra Raghuvanshi and Ors. v. Babita Raghuvanshi and Ors.

MANU/SC/0239/2013; The State of Madhya Pradesh v. Laxmi Narayan and Ors. MANU/SC/0320/2019; N.G. Dastane v. S. Dastane MANU/SC/0330/1975; V. Bhagat v. D. Bhagat MANU/SC/0155/1994; Ashok Hurra and Ors. v. Rupa Bipin Zaveri and Ors. MANU/SC/0283/1997; Naveen Kohli v. Neelu Kohli MANU/SC/1387/2006; Munish Kakkar v. Nidhi Kakkar MANU/SC/1753/2019; Sivasankaran v. Santhimeenal MANU/SC/0634/2021; R. Srinivas Kumar v. R. Shametha MANU/SC/1382/2019; Hitesh Bhatnagar v. Deepa Bhatnagar MANU/SC/0428/2011; Sureshta Devi v. Om Prakash MANU/SC/0718/1991; Smruti Pahariya v. Sanjay Pahariya MANU/SC/0980/2009; Shyam Sunder Kohli v. Sushma Kohli MANU/SC/0855/2004; Darshan Gupta v. Radhika Gupta MANU/SC/0627/2013; Gurbux Singh v. Harminder Kaur MANU/SC/0829/2010; Neelam Kumar v. Dayarani MANU/SC/0436/2010; Satish Sitole v. Ganga MANU/SC/7822/2008; Vishnu Dutt Sharma v. Manju Sharma MANU/SC/0314/2009; Savitri Pandey v. Prem Chandra Pandey MANU/SC/0010/2002; Ms Jorden Diengdeh v. S.S. Chopra MANU/SC/0195/1985; Poonam v. Sumit Tanwar MANU/SC/0187/2010; State (through) Central Bureau of Investigation v. Kalyan Singh (former CM of UP) and Ors. MANU/SC/0461/2017; A.R. Antulay v. R.S. Nayak and Ors. MANU/SC/0002/1988; Delhi Judicial Service Association, Tis Hazari Court, Delhi v. State of Gujarat and Ors. MANU/SC/0478/1991; Mohammed Anis v. Union of India (UOI) and Ors. MANU/SC/0901/1994; Jet Ply Wood Pvt. Ltd. and Ors. v. Madhukar Nowlakha MANU/SC/8079/2006; Bhagat Singh Bugga v. Dewan Jagbir Sawhney MANU/WB/0075/1941; Popular Muthiah v. State represented by Inspector of Police MANU/SC/8399/2006; Dinesh Dutt Joshi v. The State of Rajasthan and Ors. MANU/SC/0642/2001; Bhim Singh v. Kan Singh MANU/RH/0367/2003; Nagen Kundu and Ors. v. Emperor MANU/WB/0013/1934; Chhail Das v. State of Haryana MANU/PH/0198/1974; Delhi Development Authority v. Skiper Construction Company (P) Ltd. and Ors. MANU/SC/0497/1996; Sahibzada Saiyed Muhammed Amirabbas Abbasi and Ors. v. The State of Madhya Bharat and Ors. MANU/SC/0048/1960; Ujjam Bai v. State of Uttar Pradesh MANU/SC/0101/1961; Naresh Shridhar Mirajkar and Ors. v. State of Maharashtra and Ors. MANU/SC/0044/1966

Case Note:

Family - Cooling off period - Waive of - Sections 13(1)(i-a), 13-B, 13B(2) and 23(2) of Hindu Marriage Act, 1956, Articles 142 and 142(1)of Constitution of India, Section 9 of Family Courts Act, 1984, Section 89 of Code of Civil Procedure, 1908 and Sections 320 and 482 of Code of

Criminal Procedure Code, 1973 and Section 498-A of Indian Penal Code, 1860 -This Court in Neeti Malviya v. Rakesh Malviya, had doubted view expressed in Anjana Kishore v. Puneet Kishore and Manish Goel v. Rohini Goel that this Court, in exercise of the power under Article 142 of the Constitution of India, cannot reduce or waive period of six months for moving second motion as stipulated in Sub-section (2) to Section 13-B of Hindu Marriage Act, 1956 - Hence, present reference - Whether scope and ambit of power and jurisdiction of this Court under Article 142(1) of Constitution of India need any interference, and while hearing transfer petition, or in any other proceedings, this court could exercise power under Article 142(1) of Constitution of India, in view of settlement between parties, and grant decree of divorce by mutual consent dispensing with period and procedure prescribed under Section 13-B of Act and also quash and dispose of other/connected proceedings and further this Court could grant divorce in exercise of power under Article 142(1) of Constitution of India when there was complete and irretrievable breakdown of marriage in spite of other spouse opposing prayer.

Facts:

This Court in Neeti Malviya v. Rakesh Malviya, wherein a bench of two judges had doubted the view expressed in Anjana Kishore v. Puneet Kishore and Manish Goel v. Rohini Goel that this Court, in exercise of the power under Article 142 of the Constitution of India, cannot reduce or waive the period of six months for moving the second motion as stipulated in Sub-section (2) to Section 13-B of the Hindu Marriage Act, 1956. Noticing that this Court, some High Courts and even family courts in some States had been dispensing with or reducing the period of six months for moving the second motion when there was no possibility whatsoever of the spouses cohabiting, the question was referred to a three judges' bench for a clear ruling. However, the question was never decided.

Held, while answering the reference:

(i) The plenary and conscientious power conferred on this Court under Article 142(1) of the Constitution of India, seemingly unhindered, is tempered or bounded by restraint, which must be exercised based on fundamental considerations of general and specific public policy. Fundamental general conditions of public policy refer to the fundamental rights, secularism, federalism, and other basic features of the Constitution of India. Specific public policy should be understood as some express pre-eminent prohibition in any substantive law, and not stipulations and requirements to a particular statutory scheme. It should not contravene a fundamental and non-derogable principle at the core of the statute. Even in the strictest sense, it was never doubted or debated that this Court is empowered under Article 142(1) of the Constitution of India to do complete justice without being bound by the relevant provisions of procedure, if it is satisfied that the departure from the said procedure is necessary to do complete justice between the parties. Difference between procedural and substantive law in jurisprudential terms is contentious, albeit not necessary to be examined in depth in the present decision, as in terms of the dictum enunciated by this Court in Union Carbide Corporation and Supreme Court Bar Association, exercise of power under Article 142(1) of the Constitution of India to do complete justice in a cause or matter is prohibited only when the exercise is to pass an order which is plainly and expressly barred by statutory provisions of substantive law based on fundamental considerations of general or specific public policy. As explained in Supreme Court Bar Association, the exercise of power under Article 142(1) of the Constitution of India being curative in nature, this Court would not ordinarily pass an order ignoring or disregarding a statutory provision governing the subject, except to balance the equities between conflicting claims of the litigating parties by ironing out creases in a cause or matter before it. In this sense, this Court is not a forum of restricted jurisdiction when it decides and settles the dispute in a cause or matter. While this Court cannot supplant the substantive law by building a new edifice where none existed earlier, or by ignoring express substantive statutory law provisions, it is a problem-solver in the nebulous areas. As long as complete justice required by the cause or matter' is achieved without violating fundamental principles of general or specific public policy, the exercise of the power and discretion under Article 142(1) is valid and as per the Constitution of India. This is the reason why the power under Article 142(1) of the Constitution of India is undefined and uncatalogued, so as to ensure elasticity to mould relief to suit a given situation. The fact that the power is conferred only on this Court is an assurance that it will be used with due restraint and circumspection.[13]

(ii) The legislature and the courts treat matrimonial litigations as a special, if not a unique, category. Public policy underlying the legislations dealing with family and matrimonial matters is to encourage mutual settlement, as is clearly stated in Section 89 of the Code of Civil Procedure, Section 23(2) of the Hindu Marriage Act, and Section 9 of the Family Courts

Act, 1984. Given that there are multiple legislations governing different aspects, even if the cause of dispute is identical or similar, most matrimonial disputes lead to a miscellany of cases including criminal cases, at times genuine, and on other occasions initiated because of indignation, hurt, anger or even misguided advice to teach a lesson. The multiplicity of litigations can restrict and block solutions, as a settlement has to be holistic and comprehensive, given that the objective and purpose is to enable the parties to cohabit and live together, or if they decide to part ways, to have a new beginning and settle down to live peacefully. Therefore, in B.S. Joshi and Ors. v. State of Haryana and Anr, this Court, notwithstanding that Section 320 of the Code of Criminal Procedure does not permit compounding of an offence under Section 498A of the Indian Penal Code, has held that the High Court, exercising the power under Section 482 of the Code of Criminal Procedure, may quash prosecutions even in non-compoundable offences when the ends of justice so require. This view had been affirmed by the three judges' bench in Gian Singh v. State of Punjab and Anr and reiterated by another three judges bench in Jitendra Raghuvanshi and Ors. v. Babita Raghuvanshi and Anr. The reason was that the courts must not encourage matrimonial litigation, and prolongation of such litigation is detrimental to both the parties who lose their young age in chasing multiple litigations. Thus, adopting a hyper-technical view can be counter productive as pendency itself causes pain, suffering and harassment and, consequently, it is the duty of the court to ensure that matrimonial matters are amicably resolved, thereby bringing the agony, affliction, and torment to an end. In this regard, the courts only have to enquire and ensure that the settlement between the parties is achieved without pressure, force, coercion, fraud, misrepresentation, or undue influence, and that the consent is indeed sought by free will and choice, and the autonomy of the parties is not compromised. The latter two decisions in Gian Singh and Jitendra Raghuvanshi and others observe that the inherent power on the High Court under Section 482 of the Code of Criminal Procedure is wide and can be used/wielded to quash criminal proceedings to secure the ends of justice and prevent abuse of the process of the court, albeit it has to be exercised sparingly, carefully, and with caution. This Court, in State of Madhya Pradesh v. Laxmi Narayan and Ors has set out guidelines as to when the High Court may exercise jurisdiction under the inherent powers conferred under Section 482 of the Code of Criminal Procedure for quashing non-compoundable offences in terms of Section 320 of the Code of Criminal Procedure In view of the above legal position and discussion, this Court, on the basis of settlement between the parties, while passing a decree of divorce by mutual consent, could set aside and quash other proceedings and orders, including criminal cases and First Information Report(s), provided the conditions, as specified in the mentioned judgments, were satisfied. [22]

(iii) The grant of divorce on the ground of irretrievable breakdown of marriage by this Court is not a matter of right, but a discretion which is to be exercised with great care and caution, keeping in mind several factors ensuring that complete justice is done to both parties. It is obvious that this Court should be fully convinced and satisfied that the marriage is totally unworkable, emotionally dead and beyond salvation and, therefore, dissolution of marriage is the right solution and the only way forward. That the marriage has irretrievably broken down is to be factually determined and firmly established. For this, several factors are to be considered such as the period of time the parties had cohabited after marriage, when the parties had last cohabited, the nature of allegations made by the parties against each other and their family members, the orders passed in the legal proceedings from time to time, cumulative impact on the personal relationship, whether, and how many attempts were made to settle the disputes by intervention of the court or through mediation, and when the last attempt was made, etc. The period of separation should be sufficiently long, and anything above six years or more will be a relevant factor. But these facts have to be evaluated keeping in view the economic and social status of the parties, including their educational qualifications, whether the parties have any children, their age, educational qualification, and whether the other spouse and children are dependent, in which event how and in what manner the party seeking divorce intends to take care and provide for the spouse or the children. Question of custody and welfare of minor children, provision for fair and adequate alimony for the wife, and economic rights of the children and other pending matters, if any, are relevant considerations. This court would not like to codify the factors so as to curtail exercise of jurisdiction under Article 142(1) of the Constitution of India, which is situation specific. Some of the factors mentioned can be taken as illustrative, and worthy of consideration. [33]

(iv) The decisions of this Court in Manish Goel, Neelam Kumar, Darshan Gupta, Hitesh Bhatnagar, Savitri Pandey and others have to be read down in the context of the power of this Court given by the Constitution of India to do complete justice in exercise of the jurisdiction under Article 142(1) of the Constitution of India. In consonance with our findings on the scope and ambit of the power under Article 142(1) of the Constitution of India, in the context of matrimonial disputes arising out of the Hindu Marriage Act, it was held that the power to do complete justice was not fettered by the doctrine of fault and blame, applicable to petitions for divorce under Section 13(1)(i-a) of the Hindu Marriage Act. This Court's power to dissolve marriage on settlement by passing a decree of divorce by mutual consent, as well as quash and set aside other proceedings, including criminal proceedings, remains and could be exercised. [40]

(v) This court decide this reference by answering the questions framed in the following manner:

(a) The question as to the power and jurisdiction of this Court under Article 142(1) of the Constitution of India was answered, interlia, holding that this Court could depart from the procedure as well as the substantive laws, as long as the decision was exercised based on considerations of fundamental general and specific public policy. While deciding whether to exercise discretion, this Court must consider the substantive provisions as enacted and not ignore the same, albeit this Court acts as a problem solver by balancing out equities between the conflicting claims. This power was to be exercised in a cause or matter.

(b) This Court, in view of settlement between the parties, had the discretion to dissolve the marriage by passing a decree of divorce by mutual consent, without being bound by the procedural requirement to move the second motion. This power should be exercised with care and caution, keeping in mind the factors stated in Amardeep Singh and Amit Kumar. This Court could also, in exercise of power under Article 142(1) of the Constitution of India, quash and set aside other proceedings and orders, including criminal proceedings.

(c) This Court, in exercise of power under Article 142(1) of the Constitution of India, has the discretion to dissolve the marriage on the ground of its irretrievable breakdown. This discretionary power is to be exercised to do complete justice to the parties, wherein this Court is satisfied that the facts established show that the marriage has completely failed and there is no possibility that the parties will cohabit together, and continuation of the formal legal relationship is unjustified. The Court, as a court of equity, is required to also balance the circumstances and the background in which the party opposing the dissolution is placed. [42]

Ratio Decidendi:The Supreme Court, in exercise of power under Article 142(1) of the Constitution of India, has the discretion to dissolve the marriage on the ground of its irretrievable breakdown.

• • •

34

Sukhbir Singh Badal vs. Balwant Singh Khera and Ors. (28.04.2023 – SC) : MANU/SC/0484/2023

Relative Section:

Code of Criminal Procedure, 1973 (CrPC) - Section 200, Code of Criminal Procedure, 1973 (CrPC) - Section 202, Code of Criminal Procedure, 1973 (CrPC) - Section 203, Code of Criminal Procedure, 1973 (CrPC) - Section 204, Code of Criminal Procedure, 1973 (CrPC) - Section 315(1), Code of Criminal Procedure, 1973 (CrPC) - Section 482; Indian Penal Code, 1860 (IPC) - Section 120B, Indian Penal Code, 1860 (IPC) - Section 191, Indian Penal Code, 1860 (IPC) - Section 192, Indian Penal Code, 1860 (IPC) - Section 415, Indian Penal Code, 1860 (IPC) - Section 420, Indian Penal Code, 1860 (IPC) - Section 463, Indian Penal Code, 1860 (IPC) - Section 464, Indian Penal Code, 1860 (IPC) - Section 465, Indian Penal Code, 1860 (IPC) - Section 466, Indian Penal Code, 1860 (IPC) - Section 467, Indian Penal Code, 1860 (IPC) - Section 468, Indian Penal Code, 1860 (IPC) - Section 471; Information Technology Act, 2000 - Section 2; Representation Of The People Act, 1951 - Section 29A, Representation Of The People Act, 1951 - Section 29A(5)

Hon'ble Judges/Coram: M.R. Shah and C.T. Ravikumar, JJ.

Equivalent Citation: AIR2023SC3053, 2023 (2) ALT (Crl.) 176 (A.P.), 2023CriLJ2746, 2023/INSC/466

Number of Pages in the Original Judgment: 13

Case Reference:

Sardar Sarup Singh and Ors. v. State of Punjab and Ors. MANU/SC/0238/1959; S.R. Bommai and Ors. v. Union of India (UOI) and Ors. MANU/SC/0444/1994; The Commissioner, Hindu Religious Endowments, Madras v. Lakshmindra Thirtha Swamiar of Sri Shirur Mutt. MANU/SC/0136/1954; Birla Corporation Limited and Ors. v. Adventz Investments and Holdings Limited and Ors. MANU/SC/0714/2019; Md. Ibrahim and Ors. v. State of Bihar and Ors. MANU/SC/1604/2009; Sunil Bharti Mittal v. Central Bureau of Investigation MANU/SC/0016/2015; Mehmood Ul Rehman and Ors. v. Khazir Mohammad Tunda and Ors. MANU/SC/0374/2015

Case Note:

Criminal - Summoning order - Legality - Section 29-A(5) of the Representation of People Act, 1951 ("Act, 1951"); Section 482 of Code of Criminal Procedure, 1973 (CrPC) - Original Accused - Appellants have preferred the present appeals feeling dissatisfied with the impugned judgment passed by the High Court by which the High Court has dismissed the said application filed under Section 482 of CrPC and refused to quash the criminal proceedings as well as the summoning order - Whether High Court is right in refusing to quash the criminal proceedings as well as the summoning order?

Facts:

Appellants herein are summoned by the learned Trial Court to face the trial for the offences Under Sections 420, 465, 466, 467, 468, 471 read with Section 120B of IPC. The main allegation in the complaint was that in the year 1989 and as per the Constitution prevailing at the relevant time, i.e., in the year 1989, Shiromani Akali Dal (Badal) was engaged in non-secularism but they contested and got seats in the elections to the SGPC, therefore, the Memorandum annexed with the application for registration Under Section 29-A of the Act, 1951 was false.

Held, while allowing the appeal

1. From the material on record, more particularly, the application for registration of the Shiromani Akali Dal (Badal) under Section 29-A of the Act, 1951, it appears that as per the requirement under Section 29-A, that a political party should deal in secularism and socialism, a Memorandum to that effect was produced. Neither the "Constitution" of the Party nor any other "Rules or Regulations" were produced. It was stated in the application that the Party had adopted a Memorandum to the effect that "Shiromani Akali Dal (Badal) shall bear true faith and allegiance to the Constitution of India as by law established and to the principles of socialism, secularism and democracy and would uphold the sovereignty, unity and integrity of India". What was produced was the copy of the Memorandum. [5.3]

2. Looking to the averments and allegations in the complaint, it is not appreciable at all, how the Appellants are alleged to have committed the offence of cheating. The ingredients for the offence of cheating are not at all satisfied. There is no question of deceiving any person, fraudulently or dishonestly to deliver any property to any person. Therefore, even on bare reading of the averments and allegations in the complaint, no case even remotely for the offence Under Section 420 of IPC is made out. [5.6]

3. Therefore, as per Section 463, "whoever makes any false documents, with intent to cause damage or injury, to the public or to any person, or to support any claim or title, or to cause any person to part with property, or to enter into any express or implied contract, or with intent to commit fraud or that fraud may be committed", he is said to have committed the offence of forgery. Making a false document is defined Under Section 464 of IPC. Therefore, for the offence of forgery, there must be making of a false document with intent to cause damage or injury to the public or to any person. Therefore, making the false documents is sine qua non. [5.8]

4. In the present case, no false document has been produced. What was produced was the Memorandum and no other documents were produced. Even according to the original complainant, the Memorandum and the claim made at the time of registration of the Party that it has adopted a Memorandum accepting the secularism, the same was contrary to the Constitution of the Party produced before the Gurudwara Election Commission. Making a false claim and creating and producing the false document both are different and distinct. [5.9]

5. Now, so far as the offences Under Sections 466, 467, and 468 of IPC are concerned, on the face of it, it cannot be said that any case is made out for the said offences. Section 466 is with respect to forgery of record of court or of public register. Section 467 is with respect to forgery of valuable security, will etc. Section 468 relates to forgery for the purposes of cheating. Section 471 will be applicable in case of using as genuine a forged document. [5.10]

6. Looking to the averments and allegations in the complaint and even the material/evidence collected/ recorded during the course of the inquiry and even assuming the complaint's averments to be true, the ingredients of the offence punishable Under Sections 420, 465, 466, 467, 468, 471 are not at all made out. [5.11]

7. Even the application Under Section 29-A of the Act, 1951 was made as far as back in the year 1989 and thereafter even the Respondent No. 1 filed the complaint before the ECI, which came to be dismissed by the ECI and thereafter the present complaint has been filed in the year 2009, i.e., after a period of 20 years from the date of filing of the application for registration Under Section 29-A of the Act, 1951, which was made in the year 1989. [5.12]

8. Even assuming the complaint's averments to be true, do not make out the ingredients of the offences, for which the learned Trial Court has passed

the summoning order. Under the circumstances to continue the criminal proceedings against the Appellants - Accused arising out of the complaint and to face the trial by the Accused as per the summoning order is nothing but an abuse of process of law and court and this is a fit case to quash the entire criminal proceedings arising out of the complaint filed by the Respondent No. 1 including the summoning order passed by the learned Trial Court. [6]

9. The impugned judgment and order passed by the High Court dismissing the revision application is hereby quashed and set aside. The order passed by the Trial Court summoning the Appellants - Accused to face the trial for the offences Under Sections 420, 465, 466, 467, 468, 471 read with 120B of IPC is quashed and set aside. Appeals allowed. [7]

Ratio Decidendi: For the offence of forgery, there must be making of a false document with intent to cause damage or injury to the public or to any person

Disposition: Appeal Allowed.

• • •

CHAPTER XI

Bohatie Devi (Dead) through L.R. vs. The State of Uttar Pradesh and Ors. (28.04.2023 – SC) : MANU/SC/0473/2023

Relative Section:

Code of Criminal Procedure, 1973 (CrPC)-Section 158,Section 173,Section 173(3),Section 173(8),Section 482;

Indian Penal Code, 1860 (IPC) - Section 120B, Indian Penal Code, 1860 (IPC) - Section 302

Hon'ble Judges/Coram: M.R. Shah and C.T. Ravikumar, JJ.

Equivalent Citation: 2023(246)AIC108, 2023 (124) ACC 274, 136(2023)CLT246, 2023CriLJ2401, 2023/INSC/465, 2023(2)RCR(Criminal)841

Number of Pages in the Original Judgment: 8

Case Reference:

State of A.P. v. A.S. Peter MANU/SC/8222/2007; Ram Lal Narang and Ors. v. State (Delhi Administration) MANU/SC/0216/1979

Case Note:

Criminal - Investigation - Transfer thereto - Section 173 of Code of Criminal Procedure, 1973 (CrPC) - Original writ Petitioner has preferred the present appeal feeling aggrieved with the impugned judgment passed by the High Court by which, the High Court observed that, further investigation was ordered after intimation to the learned Magistrate and therefore, there is no infirmity in the order passed by the Secretary (Home) directing further investigation - Whether order passed by the Secretary (Home) impugned before the High Court, by which, the Secretary (Home), State of U.P., ordered for reinvestigation by CBCID of under Sections 302 and 120B of IPC, is liable to be quashed?

Facts:

Son of the Appellant - Satyaveer was murdered by un-known persons. An FIR was lodged by the informant son-in- law of the Appellant against Smt. Anju and two un-known persons. The investigation was carried out by the Inspector of Police, Baraut, District Baghpat who submitted chargesheet against two persons of which cognizance was taken by the learned

Magistrate on 31.03.2015. That thereafter, on the complaint/application by the Appellant, the investigation was handed over to the District Crime Branch. By order, Secretary (Home) State of U.P., Lucknow, ordered further investigation by CBCID. The order passed by the Secretary (Home) transferring investigation to CBCID was impugned before the High Court by way of present petition. By the impugned judgment and order the High Court has dismissed the writ petition by observing that further investigation was ordered after intimation to the learned Magistrate and therefore, there is no infirmity in the order passed by the Secretary (Home) directing further investigation.

Held, while allowing the appeal

1. Respondent Nos. 8 and 11 have been charge sheeted for the offence under Sections 302 and 120B of the IPC of which the cognizance has been taken by the learned Magistrate. That thereafter, Respondent No. 8 moved the quashing petition before the High Court for quashing the entire criminal proceedings including the charge sheet/supplementary charge sheet. The High Court dismissed the quashing petition. Therefore, the Accused must have taken all the defences which might have been available to him while considering quashing petition including the ground on which now further investigation/reinvestigation is ordered by another agency, namely, CBCID. It is required to be noted that thereafter, Respondent No. 8 approached this Court and the Special Leave Petition came to be dismissed by this Court and the interim protection in favour of Respondent No. 8 came to be vacated. That thereafter, non-bailable warrant was issued against Respondent No. 8 and only thereafter, mother of Respondent No. 8 - Accused moved an application before the Secretary (Home) for further investigation and he transferred the investigation to CBCID, on the ground that the so-called eye witnesses of the murder were not the eye witnesses. The request of the mother of Accused has been accepted by the Secretary (Home) and the investigation was transferred to another agency, namely, CBCID despite the fact that after the first charge sheet, the investigation was handed over to the District Crime Branch to further investigate the case and they filed the supplementary charge sheet in which Respondent Nos. 8 and 11 were even charge sheeted. Therefore, it is not a case of further investigation, but is a case of reinvestigation by another agency. The order passed by the Secretary (Home) transferring the investigation/ordering further investigation by another agency and that too, on the basis of the application/complaint submitted by mother of the Accused is un- known to

law. [7]

2. There cannot be any dispute that even after the charge sheet is filed, it is the right of the investigating officer to further investigate in respect of offence even after a report Under Sub-section (2) of Section 173 of CrPC forwarded to a Magistrate and as observed and held by this Court the prior approval of the Magistrate is not required. However, as per the settled position of law, so far as the reinvestigation is concerned, the prior permission/approval of the Magistrate is required. In the present case, the Secretary (Home) has passed an order for further investigation by CBCID and thereafter, the CBCID has sent the intimation to the learned Magistrate. No prior approval/permission as observed by the High Court has been accorded by the learned Magistrate. The High Court in the impugned judgment and order has observed that the further investigation is ordered with the concurrence of the Magistrate, which is factually incorrect. What is on record is only an intimation to the learned Magistrate which in any case cannot be said to be concurrence of the learned Magistrate. [7.1]

3. As it is a case of reinvestigation, the same is not permissible and that too by another agency without the prior permission of the learned Magistrate even while exercising the powers Under Section 173(8) of the CrPC, under what authority of law, the Secretary (Home) has transferred the investigation to another agency and/or ordered further investigation by another agency is not pointed out and that too at the instance of the Accused on the grounds which as such can be said to be the defences of the Accused which are required to be considered at the time of trial. If the Accused is aggrieved by the charge sheet in that case, the remedy available to him would be either to file the quashing petition Under Section 482 of Code of Criminal Procedure and/or to move an appropriate application for discharge before the learned Magistrate and it is for the High Court and/or the learned Magistrate as the case may be, to quash criminal proceedings or discharge the Accused. The Secretary (Home) and/or any Accused who is already charge sheeted cannot be permitted to circumvent such provision. In the present case, Respondent No. 8 - Accused earlier did file the quashing petition, but failed. [7.2]

4. Section 173(3) read with Section 158 does not permit the Secretary (Home) to order for further investigation/reinvestigation by another agency, other than the officer in charge of the concerned Police Station and/or his superior officer. [7.3]

5. The impugned judgment and order passed by the High Court is quashed and set aside. Consequently, order passed by the Secretary (Home) impugned before the High Court, by which, the Secretary (Home), State of U.P., ordered for reinvestigation by CBCID of under Sections 302 and 120B of IPC, is quashed and set aside. Appeal allowed. [8]

Ratio Decidendi: The prior permission/approval of the Magistrate is required in a case of reinvestigation.

* * *

CHAPTER XII

P.V. Nidhish and Ors. vs. Kerala State Wakf Board and Ors. (28.04.2023 – SC) : MANU/SC/0479/2023

Relative Section:

Bombay Rents, Hotel And Lodging House Rates Control Act, 1947 - Section 25 (4), Bombay Rents, Hotel And Lodging House Rates Control Act, 1947 - Section 24, Bombay Rents, Hotel And Lodging House Rates Control Act, 1947 - Section 24(1); Cattle-trespass Act, 1871 - Section 20;

Code of Civil Procedure, 1908 (CPC) - Order XXXIX Rule 1,Order XXXIX Rule 2;

Code of Criminal Procedure, 1973 (CrPC) - Section 2 (n),Section 472, Section 482;

Constitution of India - Article 20 (1), Constitution of India - Article 20(1);

Waqf Act, 1995 - Section 3 (c), Section 3 (ee), Section 52A (2), Section 52A (3), Section 3(ee), Section 13, Section 52A(1), Section 54, Section 56, Section 106

Hon'ble Judges/Coram:

S. Ravindra Bhat and Dipankar Datta, JJ.

Equivalent Citation: 2023(246)AIC120, 2023 (159) ALR 243, 2023/INSC/452, 2023(3)KLT300, 2023(3) MLJ (Crl)63, 2023(2)RCR(Criminal)833

Number of Pages in the Original Judgment: 11

Case Reference:

Mohan Lal v. State of Rajasthan MANU/SC/0465/2015; Ramesh Gobindram (Dead) through L.Rs. v. Sugra Humayun Mirza Wakf MANU/SC/0659/2010; Rao Shiv Bahadur Singh and Ors. v. The State of Vindhya Pradesh MANU/SC/0081/1953; T. Barai v. Henry Ah Hoe and Ors. MANU/SC/0123/1982; Kanaiyalal Chandulal Monim v. Indumati T. Potdar and Ors. MANU/SC/0134/1958; Norman Printing Bureau v. Mammu Haji, P.M. and Ors. MANU/KE/0787/2013

Case Note:

Criminal -Quashing of proceedings - Sections3(ee) and 52A of Wakf Act, 1995 - Criminal complaint was filed before Court of Judicial Magistrate, alleging that Appellants were encroachers and seeking their prosecution under Section 52A of Act - Appellants alleged that they continued to pay rent, in accordance with decree of District Judge - Appellants preferred petition before High Court alleging that they could not be treated as encroachers and were lawful occupants, whose eviction was sought, in civil proceedings, and seeking quashing of those proceedings - By impugned order, High Court rejected petition - Hence, present appeal - Whether impugned prosecution under Section 52A of Act required to be quashed.

Facts:

A criminal complaint was filed before the Court of the Judicial Magistrate, First Class, alleging that the Appellants were encroachers and seeking their prosecution under Section 52A. The Appellants alleged that they continued to pay the rent, in accordance with the decree of the District Judge, in their interpleader suit. The Appellants preferred a petition before the High Court alleging that they could not be treated as encroachers and were lawful occupants, whose eviction was sought, in civil proceedings, and seeking quashing of those proceedings. By the impugned order, the High Court rejected the petition.

Held, while allowing the appeal:

(i) It was undeniable that the Appellant came into possession even before the wakf was created before even the Wakf Act, 1954 was enacted. It was, however, sufficient to notice that in an interpleader suit, the Appellants were permitted to pay rents to the third Defendant in the suit. They were holding the premises when the amendment came into force indeed, a proceeding purporting to evict them was unsuccessfully initiated before the amendment. Another one was commenced and was pending after it came into force. In these circumstances, could it be said having regard to the previous discussion that the dispute over the termination of their tenancy, resulted in their becoming encroachers after the amendment became effective. [21]

(ii) The expiry of leases, or other arrangements, by efflux of time or their valid terminations, in the past, could not be construed to mean that such lessees become encroachers. Nor would past tenants whose possession is disputed, and eviction proceedings pending against them before a court, fit that description under Section 3(ee). The consequences of such an interpretation would be too startling; even before an adjudication of the validity of termination, tenants holding over would be exposed to prosecution. There was no allusion to continuing offence or any expression suggesting that such a term would be attracted to actions which commenced in the past, i.e., before the amendment of 2013 came into force. To hold otherwise, this Court would be resorting to an interpretation that directly deprives the Appellants of their rights under Article 20(1) a consequence that could not be countenanced. The plain text of that provision forbids such an interpretation, and the authorities on that aspect clearly indicate that giving effect to a penal statue so as to cover past acts was a proscribed action in law. Therefore, the expression Whoever alienates or purchases or takes possession of, which was the opening phrase of Section 52A, could not be read or construed to include possession taken in the past, which resulted in continued possession, when the provision was enacted. That was to say that Section 52A could not cover cases where leases of wakf properties had expired in the past and where the tenant or lessee was, at the time the amendment of 2013 came into force, in physical possession and facing civil proceedings for eviction. [22]

Disposition: In Favour of Accused.

• • •

CHAPTER XIII

Ajay Kumar Radheyshyam Goenka vs. Tourism Finance Corporation of India Ltd. (15.03.2023 – SC) : MANU/SC/0244/2023

Relative Section:

NEGOTIABLE INSTRUMENTS ACT, 1881 - Section 138; NEGOTIABLE INSTRUMENTS ACT, 1881 - Section 139, NEGOTIABLE INSTRUMENTS ACT, 1881 - Section 141, NEGOTIABLE INSTRUMENTS ACT, 1881 - Section 142, NEGOTIABLE INSTRUMENTS ACT, 1881 - Section 147; INSOLVENCY AND BANKRUPTCY CODE, 2016 - Section 7, INSOLVENCY AND BANKRUPTCY CODE, 2016 - Section 8, INSOLVENCY AND BANKRUPTCY CODE, 2016 - Section 9, INSOLVENCY AND BANKRUPTCY CODE, 2016 - Section 13, INSOLVENCY AND BANKRUPTCY CODE, 2016 - Section 15, INSOLVENCY AND BANKRUPTCY CODE, 2016 - Section 32A, Section 61

Hon'ble Judges/Coram:

Sanjay Kishan Kaul, Abhay Shreeniwas Oka and J.B. Pardiwala, JJ.

Equivalent Citation: [2023]237 CompCas601(SC), 2023GLH(2)385, 2023/INSC/232, 2023(2) MLJ(Crl) 417,2023 (1) MWN (Cr.) D.C.C. 145, 2023(2)RCR(Criminal)161, [2023]178SCL401(SC), 2023(2)ShimLC601

Number of Pages in the Original Judgment: 45

Case Reference:

Ajit Balse v. Ranga Karkere MANU/SC/0444/2015; P. Mohanraj and Ors. v. Shah Brothers Ispat Pvt. Ltd. MANU/SC/0132/2021; Swiss Ribbons Pvt. Ltd. and Ors. v. Union of India (UOI) and Ors. MANU/SC/0079/2019; Committee of Creditors of Essar Steel India Limited v. Satish Kumar Gupta and Ors. MANU/SC/1577/2019; Ghanashyam Mishra and Sons Private Limited v. Edelweiss Asset Reconstruction Company Limited and Ors. MANU/SC/0273/2021; Ebix Singapore Private Limited and Ors. v. Committee of Creditors of Educomp Solutions Limited and Ors. MANU/ SC/0628/2021; Manish Kumar v. Union of India (UOI) and Ors. MANU/ SC/0029/2021; Kaushalya Devi Massand v. Roopkishore Khore MANU/ SC/0385/2011; Meters and Instruments Private Limited and Ors. v. Kanchan Mehta MANU/SC/1256/2017; Aneeta Hada and Ors. v. Godfather

Travels and Tours Pvt. Ltd. and Ors. MANU/SC/0335/2012; State Bank Of India v. Bhushan Steel Limited MANU/NC/5284/2018; JIK Industries Limited and Ors. v. Amarlal V. Jumani and Ors. MANU/SC/0075/2012; Anil Hada v. Indian Acrylic Limited MANU/SC/0736/1999; State of Rajasthan and Ors. v. Shamsher Singh MANU/SC/0112/1985; Lalit Kumar Jain v. Union of India and Ors. MANU/SC/0352/2021; Maharashtra State Electricity Board, Bombay v. Official Liquidator, High Court, Ernakulam and Ors. MANU/SC/0024/1982; Jagannath Ganeshram Agarwala v. Shivnarayan Bhagirath MANU/MH/0166/1939; J.K. (Bombay) P. Ltd. v. New Kaiser-I-Hind Spg. and Wvg. Co. Ltd. and Ors. MANU/SC/0217/ 1968; Indorama Synthetics (I) Limited v. State of Maharashtra and Ors. MANU/MH/0692/2016; Narinder Garg and Ors. v. Kotak Mahindra Bank Ltd. and Ors. MANU/SC/0552/2022; Shah Brothers Ispat Pvt. Ltd. v. P. Mohan Raj and Ors. Company Appeal (AT) Insolvency No. 306 of 2018; In Re: Fitzgeorge (1905) 1 KB 462; Goa State Cooperative Bank Limited v. Krishna Nath A. and Ors. MANU/ SC/1123/2019 : (2019) 20 SCC 38; State Bank of India v. V. Ramakrishnan and Anr. MANU /SC/0849/2018 : (2018) 17 SCC 394; Vijay Kumar Jain v. Standard Chartered Bank MANU/ SC/0111/2019 : (2019) 20 SCC 455

Case Note:

Criminal - Penal liability - Prosecution against signatory- Section 138 of Negotiable Instruments Act, 1881 and Sections 9, 14, 31, 32A and 32A(1) of Insolvency and Bankruptcy Code, 2016 - Respondent-complainant had advanced sum as corporate loan to Original Accused No. 1/corporate debtor of which Appellant was managing director - Amount came to be repaid before disputes arose between parties to which complainant issued notice to corporate debtor to settle balance amount - Complaint was lodged under Section 138 of Act by complainant against corporate debtor and Appellant for dishonour of cheques issued by Appellant - One of operational creditors filed application under Section 9 of Code before NCLT seeking to initiate Corporate Insolvency Resolution Process with respect to corporate debtorwhich was admitted - Resolution applicant filed its resolution plan to which Complainant lodged his objections before NCLT in so far as it changed its status from secured to unsecured creditor - In meantime, Appellant preferred application before trial court seeking exemption from his personal appearance invoking moratorium under Section 14 of IBC -Magistrate rejected said application on ground that criminal proceedings under NI Act had nothing to do with proceedings under IBC - NCLT approved resolution plan so far as corporate debtor was concernedand thereafter, Appellant filed application before trial court, praying that he be discharged from criminal proceedings - Trial court rejectedsaid application on ground that it had no jurisdiction to discharge Accused in summons triable case-Thereafter, Appellant filed revision application which stand dismissed by Additional Sessions Courtand same was upheld by High Court - Hence, present appeal - Whether in light of complainant having participated in proceedings under IBC, 2016 by putting forward its claim and consenting to accept some share as creditor coupled with approval of resolution plan under Section 31 of IBC, 2016, signatory/director in charge of day-to-day affairs would stand discharged from penal liability under Section 138 of NI Act.

Facts:

Respondent-complainant had advanced a sum as a corporate loan to the Original Accused No. 1/corporate debtor. The Appellant at the relevant point of time was the Managing Director of the company i.e. the corporate debtor. An amount came to be repaid before the disputes arose between the parties. The complainant issued a notice to the corporate debtor to settle the balance amount. A complaint was lodged under Section 138 of the NI Act by the complainant against the corporate debtor and the Appellant for dishonour of the three cheques issued by the Appellant. One of the operational creditors filed an application under Section 9 of the Insolvency and Bankruptcy Code, 2016 before the NCLT seeking to initiate Corporate Insolvency Resolution Process with respect to the corporate debtor.The Insolvency application came to be admitted by the NCLT. The complainant filed its claim before the IRP. The resolution applicant filed its resolution plan under the terms of which, the payment to the complainant was in full and final settlement of all its claims against the corporate debtor. The Committee of Creditorsapproved the resolution plan proposed by the resolution applicant. The complainant lodged his objections before the NCLT to the resolution plan in so far as it changed its status from secured to unsecured creditor. In the meantime, the Appellant preferred an application before the trial court seeking exemption from his personal appearance invoking a moratorium under Section 14 of the IBC. The Magistrate rejected the said application on the ground that the criminal proceedings under the NI Act had nothing to do with the proceedings under the IBC. The NCLT approved the resolution plan so far as the corporate debtor was concerned.As the resolution plan came to be approved by the NCLT, the

Appellant herein filed an application before the trial court, praying that he be discharged from the criminal proceedings. The trial court rejected the said application essentially on the ground that it had no jurisdiction to discharge an Accused in a summons triable case. Thereafter, the Appellant filed the Criminal Revision Application before the Additional Sessions Court, challenging the order passed by the Magistrate which stand dismissed and same was upheld by the High Court.

Held, while dismissing the appeal:

Sanjay Kishan Kaul, J.

(i) The scope of nature of proceedings under the two Acts and quite different and would not intercede each other. In fact, a bare reading of Section 14 of the IBC would make it clear that the nature of proceedings which have to be kept in abeyance do not include criminal proceedings, which is the nature of proceedings under Section 138 of the N.I. Act. This court were unable to appreciate the plea of the Appellant that because Section 138 of the N.I. Act proceedings arise from a default in financial debt, the proceedings under Section 138 should be taken as akin to civil proceedings rather than criminal proceedings. This court could not lose sight of the fact that Section 138 of the N.I. Act were not recovery proceedings. They were penal in character. A person may face imprisonment or fine or both under Section 138 of the N.I. Act. It was not a recovery of the amount with interest as a debt recovery proceedings would be. They were not akin to suit proceedings. [16]

(ii) This court were unable to accept the plea that if proceedings against the company come to an end then the Appellant as the Managing Director cannot be proceeded against. This court were unable to accept the plea that Section 138 of the N.I. Act proceedings were primarily compensatory in nature and that the punitive element was incorporated only at enforcing the compensatory proceedings. The criminal liability and the fines were built on the principle of not honouring a negotiable instrument, which affects trade. This was apart from the principle of financial liability per se. To say that under a scheme which may be approved, a part amount will be recovered or if there is no scheme a person may stand in a queue to recover debt would absolve the consequences under Section 138 of the N.I. Act, was unacceptable. [18]

J.B. Pardiwala, J.

(i) It was evident that the creditor had no option but to join the process under the IBC. Once the plan was approved, it would bind everyone under the sun. The making of a claim and accepting whatever share is allotted could be termed as an Involuntary Act on behalf of the creditor. The making of a claim under the IBC and accepting the same and not making any claim, would not make any difference in light of Section 31 of the IBC. Both the situations would lead to Section 31and the finality and binding value of the resolution plan. [61]

(ii) Where the proceedings under Section 138 of the NI Act had already commenced and during the pendency the plan was approved or the company gets dissolved, the directors and the other Accused could not escape from their liability by citing its dissolution. What is dissolved is only the company, not the personal penal liability of the Accused covered under Section 14 of the NI Act. They will have to continue to face the prosecution in view of the law laid down in Aneeta Hada. Where the company continues to remain even at the end of the resolution process, the only consequence is that the erstwhile directors can no longer represent it. [73]

(iii) As per Section 138 of the NI Act, when the cheque was dishonoured and a statutory notice demanding the cheque amount was issued, the Accused shall pay the cheque amount within fifteen days from the date of receipt of the said notice. The moment the said fifteen days expired, the cause of action arises. In other words, the offence under Section 138 of the NI Act is complete. Once the cause of action arose for the offence committed, the complainant has to approach the criminal court within one month to take penal action under Section 138 of the NI Act. To put it clearly, the complainant approaches the criminal court not for recovery of the legally enforceable debt, but for taking penal action under Section 138 of the NI Act for the offence already committed by the Accused by not making the payment of the cheque amount despite the receipt of the statutory notice. The only question before the criminal court was whether the cheque issued by the Accused towards the discharge of his liability was dishonoured and despite the service of demand notice, whether he had not paid the amount. There was no bar contained in any of the provisions of the IBC, and the NI Act from approaching the criminal court to seek penal action under Section 138 of the NI Act. [96]

(iv) This court may draw final conclusions as under:

(a) After passing of the resolution plan under Section 31 of the IBC by the adjudicating authority and in the light of the provisions of Section 32A of the IBC, the criminal proceedings under Section 138 of the NI Act will stand terminated only in relation to the corporate debtor if the same was taken over by a new management.

(b) Section 138 proceedings in relation to the signatories/directors who are liable/covered by the two provisos to Section 32A(1) would continue in accordance with law. [107]

Disposition: In Favour of State.

• • •

CHAPTER XIV

S. Athilakshmi vs. The State Rep. by the Drugs Inspector (15.03.2023 – SC) : MANU/SC/0239/

Relative Section:

Code of Criminal Procedure, 1973 (CrPC) - Section 197, Code of Criminal Procedure, 1973 (CrPC) - Section 482; Drugs And Cosmetics Act, 1940 - Section 18, Drugs And Cosmetics Act, 1940 - Section 18(c), Drugs And Cosmetics Act, 1940 - Section 18A, Drugs And Cosmetics Act, 1940 - Section 27, Drugs And Cosmetics Act, 1940 - Section 27(a), Drugs And Cosmetics Act, 1940 - Section 27(b), Drugs And Cosmetics Act, 1940 - Section 33, Drugs And Cosmetics Act, 1940 - Section 38; Drugs and Cosmetics Rules, 1940; Drugs And Cosmetics Rules, 1945 - Rule 123

Hon'ble Judges/Coram:

Krishna Murari and Sudhanshu Dhulia, JJ.

Equivalent Citation: 2023(245)AIC75, 2023 (123) ACC 977, 2023 (2) ALT (Crl.) 71 (A.P.), 2023(2)Crimes107(SC), 2023(3)CTC822, 2023/INSC/237, 2023(2)MLJ(Crl)359, [2023]2SCR914, 2023(1)ShimLC354

Number of Pages in the Original Judgment: 10

Case Reference:

Mansukhlal Vithaldas Chauhan v. State of Gujarat MANU/SC/1303/1997; Hasmukhlal D. Vohra and Ors. v. The State of Tamil Nadu MANU/SC/1639/2022; Mohd. Shabir v. State of Maharashtra MANU/SC/0182/1979

Case Note:

Criminal - Sale of medicines - Quashing of proceedings - Sections 18, 18-A, 18(c), 27 and 27(b)(ii) of Drugs and Cosmetics Act 1940 and Rule 123 of Drugs and Cosmetics Rules, 1940 - Appellant was registered medical practitioner who was working as Associate Professor and Head of Dermatology Department in Government Medical College - Appellant, in her individual and independent capacity was carrying on her medical practice at premises - Inspection was made on said premises by Drugs Inspector and found medicines in inner room of her premises - Drugs Inspector filed complaint before Court of Metropolitan Magistrate for prosecuting Appellant under Section 18(c) of Actpunishable under Section 27(b)(ii) of Act - Aggrieved by said proceedings, Appellant filed application before High Court for quashing criminal proceedings which stand dismissed - Hence, present appeal -Whether proceedings initiated against Appellant under Section 18(c) of Act liable to quashed.

Facts:

The Appellant was a registered medical practitioner who was presently working as an Associate Professor and the Head of Dermatology Department, in the Government Medical College. In the past, she has held the post of Assistant Professor and Civil Surgeon at Medical College. It was permissible for her under the law to practice medicine when she was not performing her official duties. The Appellant, in her individual and independent capacity was carrying on her medical practice at a premises. An inspection was made on the said premises by the Drugs Inspector in which found the medicines in the inner room of her premises.Consequently, the Drugs Inspector filed a complaint before the Court of Metropolitan Magistrate for prosecuting the Appellant under Section 18(c) of the Drugs and Cosmetics Act, 1940 punishable under Section 27(b)(ii) of the Act.Aggrieved by these proceedings, the Appellant filed an application before the High Court for quashing the criminal proceedings. Her petition was dismissed by theSingle Judge.

Held, while allowing the appeal:

(i) Considering the small quantity of medicines, most of which were in the category of lotions and ointments, it could not be said by any stretch of imagination that such medicines could be stocked for sale and would come in the category of stocking of medicines for the purpose of sale. When small quantity of medicine has been found in the premises of a registered medical practitioner, it would not amount to selling their medicines across the counter in an open shop. In fact, this was not even the allegation against the Appellant. Undoubtedly, the provisions of Section 18 and 27 were relevant provisions under the law, which have a social purpose, which was to protect ordinary citizens from being exploited inter alia, by unethical medical practitioners, and for this reason the punishment under Section 27 could extend up to five years under the law, and had a minimum punishment of three years. But given the facts and circumstances of the case and considering that the Appellant was a registered medical practitioner, along with the fact that the quantity of medicines which had been seized was extremely small, a quantity which could be easily found in the house or a consultation room of a doctor, no offence was made out in the present case. In fact, an exception had been created under ScheduleK read with Rule

123 to the Rules, the Appellant ought to have been given the benefit of these provisions and such a registered medical practitioner should not have been allowed to face a trial where in all likelihood the prosecution would have failed to prove its case beyond reasonable doubt. [9]

(ii) But what the High Court failed to consider, however, was the provisions contained in Rule 123 read with Schedule K to the 1945 Rules and when admittedly it was not the case of the prosecution that the drugs which were seized were being sold in an open shop across the counter. Since this was not being done as visualized above, and an exception was created under the law in favour of the medical practitioner where the drugs given in Schedule K would be exempted from the purview of Chapter 4 of the Act, it was of the view that prosecution against the Appellant was unwarranted. [10]

(iii) Upon being served with the Show Cause Notice, the Appellant was directed, under Section 18-A, to reveal the name and addresses of persons from whom she obtained the drugs which were seized. In compliance with the same, Appellant had produced multiple invoices from pharmaceutical shops to show her bonafides. Further, upon inspection of the drugs by the Drugs Testing Laboratory they returned a finding that the drugs were of standard quality which indicates it was not a case where the Appellant was operating a shop to sell spurious medicines over the counter. [12]

(iv) The sanctioning authority had not examined at all whether a practising doctor could be prosecuted under the facts of the case, considering the small quantity of the drugs and the exception created in favour of medical practitioner under Rule 123, read with the Schedule K. All these factors ought to have been considered by the sanctioning authority. Under these circumstances,set aside the order of the Single Judge of the High Court and quash the criminal proceedings. [16]

Disposition: In Favour of Accused.

• • •

CHAPTER XV

Devendra Nath Singh vs. State of Bihar and Ors. (12.10.2022 – SC) : MANU/SC/1306/2022

Relative Section:

Code of Criminal Procedure, 1973 (CrPC)-Section 2(h),Section 156,Section 156(1), Section 156(3), Section 170, Section 173, Section 173(2), Section 173(3), Section 173(4), Section 173(5), Section 173(6), Section 173(8), Section 190, Section 190(1), Section 190(2), Section 200, Section 202, Section 203,Section 204, Section 228, Section 319, Section 401, Section 401(2), Section 482;

Constitution of India - Article 21, Article 32, Article 136, Article 226;

Indian Penal Code, 1860 (IPC) - Section 302, Section 376, Section 376A, Section 376AB, Section 376B, Section 376C, Section 376D, Section 376DA, Section 376DB, Section 376E, Section 409, Section 420, Section 467, Section 468, Section 471, Section 474

Hon'ble Judges/Coram: Dinesh Maheshwari and Aniruddha Bose, JJ.

Equivalent Citation: 2023(1)ACR880, 2023(242)AIC209, AIR2022SC5344, 2023 (1) ALD(Crl.) 230 (SC), 2023 (1) ALD(Crl.) 230 (SC), 2023 (123) ACC 254, 2022(6)BLJ174, 2022(4)Crimes447(SC), 2022/INSC/1071, 2022(4)J.L.J.R.273, 2022(4)PLJR163, (2023)1SCC48

Number of Pages in the Original Judgment: 26

Case Reference:

Dharam Pal and Ors. v. State of Haryana and Ors. MANU/SC/0720/2013; Abhinandan Jha and Ors. v. Dinesh Mishra MANU/SC/0054/1967; Vinubhai Haribhai Malaviya and Ors. v. The State of Gujarat and Ors. MANU/SC/1427/2019; Madan Mohan v. State of Rajasthan and Ors. MANU/SC/1599/2017; Popular Muthiah v. State represented by Inspector of Police MANU/SC/8399/2006; Divine Retreat Centre v. State of Kerala and Ors. MANU/SC/1150/2008; Union of India (UOI) and Ors. v. W.N. Chadha MANU/SC/0149/1993; Manharibhai Muljibhai Kakadia and Ors. v. Shaileshbhai Mohanbhai Patel and Ors. MANU/SC/0819/2012; Vinay Tyagi v. Irshad Ali and Ors. MANU/SC/1101/2012; Neetu Kumar Nagaich v. The State of Rajasthan and Ors. MANU/SC/0690/2020; Disha v. State of Gujarat and Ors. MANU/SC/0841/2011; Vineet Narain and Ors. v. Union of India

(UOI) and Ors. MANU/SC/0827/1998; Union of India (UOI) and Ors. v. Sushil Kumar Modi and Ors. MANU/SC/0086/1997; Rubabbuddin Sheikh v. State of Gujarat and Ors. MANU/SC/0024/2010; Mithabhai Pashabhai Patel and Ors. v. State of Gujarat MANU/SC/0858/2009; Ramachandran v. R. Udhayakumar and Ors. MANU/SC/7684/2008; State of Punjab v. Central Bureau of Investigation and Ors. MANU/SC/1007/2011 : (2011) 9 SCC 182

Case Note:

Criminal - Inherent powers - Direction to investigate - Section 482 of Code of Criminal Procedure, 1973 (CrPC) - Challenge in present appeal is to the order as passed by the High Court relating to the direction to investigate the case in terms of Section 173(8) of CrPC regarding the allegations against the Appellant - Whether the High Court, in the exercise of its inherent powers under Section 482 of Code of Criminal Procedure, was justified in issuing directions to the Magistrate to order further investigation though, the Magistrate before whom the charge-sheet had been filed and who had taken cognizance, did not adopt any such process; and second, as to whether the High Court was justified in passing the order impugned without affording an opportunity of hearing to the Appellant?

Facts:

Petition Under Section 482 of the Code of Criminal Procedure, 1973 was filed by Respondent No. 3 of the present appeal, against the order as passed by the ACJM, whereby, the learned Magistrate had taken cognizance of the offences Under Sections 409, 467, 468 and 420 of the Indian Penal Code, 1860 on the allegations against the Respondent No. 3 of misappropriation of stocks worth Rs. 16,99,648 from the godown of the Bihar State Food and Civil Supplies Corporation during the years 2010-11 and 2011-12. High Court proceeded to direct the Magistrate to give directions to the police to further investigate the case in terms of Section 173(8) of CrPC regarding the allegations against the Appellant and to seek the report within a period of three months. The Court, however, expressed its disinclination to interfere with the impugned order taking cognizance against the present Respondent No. 3 and disposed of the petition while giving liberty to the Respondent No. 3 to raise all the points at the time of framing the charge which, as per the directions of the High Court, were to be decided by the learned Magistrate after taking into consideration the material emerging in further investigation against the Appellant. The order aforesaid is questioned by the Appellant in whose relation the directions have been issued for further investigation, inter alia, on the ground that investigation is the prcrogative of the investigating agency/officer and no mandate could be issued to the Magistrate so as to usurp such powers to investigate. It is also submitted that the impugned order has been directly in violation of the principles of natural justice inasmuch as no opportunity of hearing was extended by the High Court to the Appellant.

Held, while dismissing the appeal

1. The scheme of the Code of Criminal Procedure, 1973 is to ensure a fair trial and that would commence only after a fair and just investigation. The ultimate aim of every investigation and inquiry, whether by the police or by the Magistrate, is to ensure that the actual perpetrators of the crime are correctly booked and the innocents are not arraigned to stand trial. The powers of the Magistrate to ensure proper investigation in terms of Section 156 Code of Criminal Procedure have been recognised, which, in turn, include the power to order further investigation in terms of Section 173(8) Code of Criminal Procedure after receiving the report of investigation. Whether further investigation should or should not be ordered is within the discretion of the Magistrate, which is to be exercised on the facts of each case and in accordance with law. Even when the basic power to direct further investigation in a case where a charge-sheet has been filed is with the Magistrate, and is to be exercised subject to the limitations of Section 173(8) Code of Criminal Procedure, in an appropriate case, where the High Court feels that the investigation is not in the proper direction and to do complete justice where the facts of the case so demand, the inherent powers Under Section 482 Code of Criminal Procedure could be exercised to direct further investigation or even reinvestigation. The provisions of Section 173(8) Code of Criminal Procedure do not limit or affect such powers of the High Court to pass an order Under Section 482 Code of Criminal Procedure for further investigation or reinvestigation, if the High Court is satisfied that such a course is necessary to secure the ends of justice. Even when the wide powers of the High Court in terms of Section 482 Code of Criminal Procedure are recognised for ordering further investigation or reinvestigation, such powers are to be exercised sparingly, with circumspection, and in exceptional cases. The powers Under Section 482 Code of Criminal Procedure are not unlimited or untrammelled and are essentially for the purpose of real and substantial justice. While exercising such powers, the High Court cannot issue directions so as to be impinging upon the power and jurisdiction of other authorities. For example, the High Court cannot issue directions to the State to take advice of the State Public

Prosecutor as to under what provision of law a person is to be charged and tried when ordering further investigation or reinvestigation; and it cannot issue directions to investigate the case only from a particular angle. In exercise of such inherent powers in extraordinary circumstances, the High Court cannot specifically direct that as a result of further investigation or reinvestigation, a particular person has to be prosecuted. [13]

2. In relation to the allegations of defalcation of goods and misappropriation of stocks from the godown of the Corporation, the person lodging the FIR with reference to the audit report, i.e., the Senior Dy. Collector-cum-District Manager, made imputations only against the Respondent No. 3, who was a class IV employee of the Corporation but was purportedly posted as an in-charge Assistant Godown Manager by the Appellant, who was, at the relevant time, holding the position of the District Manager. Though several features of the actions and omissions at the relevant time have been mentioned in the audit report, we do not propose to dilate on the same. Suffice it to observe for the present purpose that when all the relevant aspects were duly projected before the High Court in the petition filed by the Respondent No. 3, the High Court could not have simply ignored the same only for the reasons that the informant omitted to state them while lodging the FIR, and/or the investigating officer overlooked them while submitting the result of investigation, and/or the learned Magistrate did not pay requisite attention to them while taking cognizance. [14]

3. In the given set of facts and circumstances, present Court is satisfied that the present one had been such a case of exceptional and special features where the High Court was justified in ordering further investigation, particularly qua the role of the Appellant. Thus, the principal part of the order impugned, directing further investigation, calls for no interference. [14.1]

4. However, there are certain other aspects and features of the order impugned which are difficult to be appreciated and approved. The High Court has chosen to use such harsh and severe expressions in the impugned order which carry all the potential of causing prejudice to the Appellant and even to distract a fair and dispassionate investigation. As noticed, the High Court has made its comments that the 'entire game was played' by the Appellant who was holding the position of District Manager. The High Court has even stated that the Appellant was 'ultimately responsible for all such irregularities'. The High Court has gone to the extent of observing that

the Respondent No. 3 was made an Accused in the case 'as scapegoat to save the skin' of the Appellant. These and other akin observations in the order impugned lead to the position as if the High Court has already concluded on the result of investigation against the Appellant. It is entirely a different matter to order further investigation on being prima facie satisfied about the requirement to do so in view of exceptional circumstances pertaining to a given case but, while doing so in exercise of inherent powers, the High Court has not been justified in making such observations and remarks which are likely to operate over and above the investigation and may cause prejudice to the Appellant. As noticed, the principle remains settled that the High Court cannot issue directions to investigate the case from a particular angle. [15]

5. Thus, in the given set of facts and circumstances, though the High Court has rightly exercised its powers Under Section 482 of CrPC for directing further investigation but, has not been justified in making such observations, comments, and remarks, which leave little scope for an independent investigation and which carry all the potential to cause prejudice to the Appellant. [16]

6. Even if the Appellant had been exonerated in the departmental proceedings, such a fact, by itself, may not be conclusive of criminal investigation; and for this fact alone, the High Court could not have ignored all other features of the case and the material factors that had surfaced before it. [19.1]

7. The entire matter is left open for examination by the investigating agency, by the sanctioning authority, and by the Court concerned at the relevant stage and in accordance with law. [21]

8. Appeal dismissed. [22]

Ratio Decidendi: In an appropriate case, where the High Court feels that the investigation is not in the proper direction, the inherent powers under Section 482 of CrPC could be exercised to direct further investigation or even reinvestigation

Disposition: In Favour of State.

● ● ●

CHAPTER XVI

S.P. Mani and Mohan Dairy vs. Snehalatha Elangovan (16.09.2022 – SC) : MANU/SC/1189/2022

Relative Section:

Code of Criminal Procedure, 1973 (CrPC) - Section 357, Code of Criminal Procedure, 1973 (CrPC) - Section 482; Companies Act, 1956 - Section 2(24), Companies Act, 1956 - Section 5; Negotiable Instruments (Amendment and Miscellaneous Provisions) Act, 2002; Negotiable Instruments Act, 1881 - Section 138, Negotiable Instruments Act, 1881 - Section 141, Negotiable Instruments Act, 1881 - Section 141(1), Negotiable Instruments Act, 1881 - Section 141(2), Negotiable Instruments Act, 1881 - Section 142

Hon'ble Judges/Coram: Surya Kant and J.B. Pardiwala, JJ.

Equivalent Citation: AIR2022SC4883, 2023 (1) ALD(Crl.) 1 (SC), 2022 (3) ALT (Crl.) 193 (A.P.), IV(2022)BC609(SC), 2022(4)CivilCC(S.C.), [2022]235CompCas212(SC), 2022(4)Crimes67(SC), 2022 (4) CriminalCC230, 2023(1)ICC32, 2022/INSC/970, 2023(1)JKJ249[SC], 2022 (6) KHC 215, 2023(1)KLJ443, 2022 (3) MWN (Cr.) D.C.C. 51, 2023(1)N.C.C.444, 2022(4)RCR(Criminal)743, [2023]175SCL242(SC), 2022(3)UC1925

Number of Pages in the Original Judgment: 22

Case Reference:

S.M.S. Pharmaceuticals Ltd. v. Neeta Bhalla and Ors. MANU/SC/0622/2005; Gunmala Sales Private Ltd. v. Anu Mehta MANU/SC/0959/2014; National Small Industries Corp. Ltd. v. Harmeet Singh Paintal and Ors. MANU/SC/0112/2010; Municipal Corporation of Delhi v. Ram Kishan Rohtagi and Ors. MANU/SC/0094/1982; U.P. Pollution Control Board v. Modi Distillery and Ors. MANU/SC/0912/1987; P. Rajarathinam v. State of Maharashtra and Ors. MANU/SC/2047/1998; K. Bhaskaran v. Sankaran Vaidhyan Balan and Ors. MANU/SC/0625/1999; N. Rangachari v. Bharat Sanchar Nigam Ltd. MANU/SC/7316/2007; Anil Hada v. Indian Acrylic Limited MANU/SC/0736/1999;Monaben Ketanbhai Shah and Ors. v. State of Gujarat and Ors. MANU/SC/0596/2004; The Assistant Commissioner, Assessment-II, Bangalore and Ors. v. Velliappa Textiles Ltd. and Ors.

MANU/SC/0721/2003; Sabitha Ramamurthy and Ors. v. R.B.S. Channabasavaradhya MANU/SC/8486/2006; K.K. Ahuja v. V.K. Vora and Ors. MANU/SC/1111/2009; Ashutosh Ashok Parasrampuriya and Ors. v. Gharrkul Industries Pvt. Ltd. and Ors. MANU/SC/0838/2021; S.K. Alagh v. State of U.P. and Ors. MANU/SC/7162/2008; Maharashtra State Electricity Distribution Co. Ltd. and Ors. v. Datar Switchgear Ltd. and Ors. MANU/SC/0815/2010; GHCL Employees Stock Option Trust v. India Infoline Ltd. MANU/SC/0271/2013; Rallis India Ltd. v. Poduru Vidya Bhusan and Ors. MANU/SC/0422/2011; Sunita Palita and Ors. v. Panchami Stone Quarry MANU/SC/0944/2022

Case Note:

Criminal - Quashing of proceedings - Challenge thereto - Section 138 of the Negotiable Instruments Act, 1881 ("the NI Act") - Present appeal is at the instance of the original complainant of a complaint filed under Section 138 of the NI Act and is directed against the order passed by the High Court, whereby the High Court allowed the application and quashed the criminal proceedings initiated against the Respondent - Whether the High Court committed any error in passing the impugned order and quashing the proceedings? Facts: The Respondent herein preferred an application under 482 of the Code of Criminal Procedure, 1973 (CrPC) in the High Court and prayed that the criminal proceedings instituted against her may be quashed as she has no liability under the law. The principal argument of the Respondent herein before the High Court was that much before the cheque came to be issued, the firm had been dissolved. The accounts of the firm were also settled on 13-02-2017 following the dissolution. The High Court quashed the proceedings against the Respondent herein mainly on the ground that there was nothing to indicate as to how and in what manner the Respondent at the relevant point of time was in-charge and responsible for the conduct of the business of the firm. The High Court took the view that the complaint can be prosecuted as against the Respondent herein only if the allegations made in the complaint fulfils the requirements of Section 141 of the NI Act. The High Court took the view that merely by reciting the words used Under Section 141 of the NI Act in the complaint no vicarious liability can be fastened on the partner of the firm. The High Court allowed the application filed by Respondent herein and terminated the proceedings as far as the Respondent is concerned. Held, while allowing the appeal 1. Once the necessary averments are made in the statutory notice issued by the complainant in regard to the vicarious liability of the partners and upon receipt of such notice, if the partner keeps quiet and does not say anything in reply to the same, then the complainant has all the reasons to believe that what he has stated in the notice has been accepted by the noticee. [45]

2. When in view of the basic averment process is issued the complaint must proceed against the Directors or partners as the case may be. But, if any Director or Partner wants the process to be quashed by filing a petition Under Section 482 of the CrPC on the ground that only a bald averment is made in the complaint and that he is really not concerned with the issuance of the cheque, he must in order to persuade the High Court to quash the process either furnish some sterling incontrovertible material or acceptable circumstances to substantiate his contention. He must make out a case that making him stand the trial would be an abuse of process of court. He cannot get the complaint quashed merely on the ground that apart from the basic averment no particulars are given in the complaint about his role, because ordinarily the basic averment would be sufficient to send him to trial and it could be argued that his further role could be brought out in the trial. Quashing of a complaint is a serious matter. Complaint cannot be quashed for the asking. For quashing of a complaint, it must be shown that no offence is made out at all against the Director or Partner. [46]

3. The primary responsibility of the complainant is to make specific averments in the complaint so as to make the Accused vicariously liable. For fastening the criminal liability, there is no legal requirement for the complainant to show that the Accused partner of the firm was aware about each and every transaction. On the other hand, the first proviso to Sub-section (1) of Section 141 of the Act clearly lays down that if the Accused is able to prove to the satisfaction of the Court that the offence was committed without his/her knowledge or he/she had exercised due diligence to prevent the commission of such offence, he/she will not be liable of punishment. The complainant is supposed to know only generally as to who were in charge of the affairs of the company or firm, as the case may be. The other administrative matters would be within the special knowledge of the company or the firm and those who are in charge of it. In such circumstances, the complainant is expected to allege that the persons named in the complaint are in charge of the affairs of the company/firm. It is only the Directors of the company or the partners of the firm, as the case may be, who have the special knowledge about the role they had played in the company or the partners in a firm to show before the court that at the relevant point of time they were not in charge of the affairs of the

company. Advertence to Sections 138 and Section 141 respectively of the NI Act shows that on the other elements of an offence Under Section 138 being satisfied, the burden is on the Board of Directors or the officers in charge of the affairs of the company/partners of a firm to show that they were not liable to be convicted. The existence of any special circumstance that makes them not liable is something that is peculiarly within their knowledge and it is for them to establish at the trial to show that at the relevant time they were not in charge of the affairs of the company or the firm. The final judgment and order would depend on the evidence adduced. Criminal liability is attracted only on those, who at the time of commission of the offence, were in charge of and were responsible for the conduct of the business of the firm. But vicarious criminal liability can be inferred against the partners of a firm when it is specifically averred in the complaint about the status of the partners 'qua' the firm. This would make them liable to face the prosecution but it does not lead to automatic conviction. Hence, they are not adversely prejudiced if they are eventually found to be not guilty, as a necessary consequence thereof would be acquittal. If any Director wants the process to be quashed by filing a petition under Section 482 of the CrPC on the ground that only a bald averment is made in the complaint and that he/she is really not concerned with the issuance of the cheque, he/she must in order to persuade the High Court to quash the process either furnish some sterling incontrovertible material or acceptable circumstances to substantiate his/her contention. He/she must make out a case that making him/her stand the trial would be an abuse of process of Court. [47]

4. Appeal allowed. [48]

Disposition: Appeal Allowed

Facts:

1. The facts of this case are plain and simple. The Appellant herein (original complainant) is engaged in the business of milk and milk products. The Respondent herein is one of the partners of a Partnership Firm running in the name of Sira Marketing Services. The firm used to purchase milk and milk products from the Appellant/complainant on credit basis. The Appellant has to recover an amount of Rs. 10,71,434.60/- (Rs. Ten Lakh Seventy One Thousand Four Hundred Thirty Four and Sixty paise) from the partnership firm. The firm issued a cheque duly signed by the original Accused No. 02 (partner/authorised signatory) in favour of the Appellant for the amount of Rs. 10,00,000/- (Rs. Ten Lakh only) dated 05.05.2017.

The cheque came to be dishonoured as there was no sufficient balance in the account maintained by the firm. No sooner, the bank intimated the Appellant herein that the cheque could not be cleared due to insufficient funds than the Appellant herein issued a statutory notice dated 14-08-2017 to the firm and the two partners of the firm. Despite service of notice to the firm as well as the two partners (Accused persons) the amount was not paid to the Appellant and therefore, the Appellant was left with no other option but to file the complaint in the Judicial Magistrate Fast Track Court No. II, Erode for the offence punishable Under Section 138 r/w 141 of the NI Act which came to registered as the STC No. 583 of 2017.[4]

Held, while allowing the appeal

1. We reiterate the observations made by this Court almost a decade back in the case of Rallis India Ltd. v. Poduru Vidya Bhusan and Ors., MANU/SC/0422/2011 : (2011) 13 SCC 88, as to how the High Court should exercise its power to quash the criminal proceeding when such proceeding is related to offences committed by the companies. "The world of commercial transactions contains numerous unique intricacies, many of which are yet to be statutorily regulated. More particularly, the principle laid down in Section 141 of the NI Act (which is pari materia with identical Sections in other Acts like the Food Safety and Standards Act, 2006; the erstwhile Prevention of Food Adulteration Act, 1954; etc.) is susceptible to abuse by unscrupulous companies to the detriment of unsuspecting third parties."[48]

2. In the result, this appeal succeeds and is hereby allowed with no order as to costs. The impugned order passed by the High Court is hereby set aside.[49]

3. Pending application, if any, also stands disposed of.[50]

• • •

CHAPTER XVII

Kaushal Kishor vs. State of Uttar Pradesh and Ors. (03.01.2023 – SC) : MANU/SC/0004/2023

Relative Section:

Bill of Rights of Final Constitution of 1996; Cable Television Networks Rules, 1994 - Rule 6, Cable Television Networks Rules, 1994 - Rule 7; Cinematograph Act, 1952 - Section 6(1); Citizenship Act, 1955 - Section 5(1); Code of Criminal Procedure, 1898 (CrPC) - Section 491; Code of Criminal Procedure, 1973 (CrPC) - Section 95, Section 154Section 482;

Constitution (First Amendment) Act, 1951 - Section 3(1); Constitution (First Amendment) Bill, 1951; Constitution (Sixteenth Amendment) Act, 1963; Constitution of India - Article 51A,Article 51A (e), Article 12, Article 13, Article 13(2), Article 14, Article 15, Article 15(1), Article 15(2), Article 16,Article 16(1), Article 16(2), Article 17, Article 19, Article 19(1), Article 19(2), Article 19(6), Article 20, Article 20(2), Article 20(3), Article 21, Article 21A, Article 22, Article 22(3), Article 23, Article 23(1), Article 24, Article 25, Article 25(1), Article 26, Article 27, Article 28(1), Article 28(3),Article 29(1),Article 29(2), Article 30,Article 30(1), Article 30(2),Article 31(1),Article 32,Article 32(2), Article 38,Article 74,Article 74(2), Article 75, Article 75(2), Article 75(3), Article 75(4), Article 77, Article 77(1), Article 77(2), Article 77(3),Article 78, Constitution Article 104Article 105, Article 131, Article 142, Article 142(1), Article 163, Article 164,Article 164(2), Article 164(3), Article 166, Article 166(1), Article 166(3), Article 167,Article 226,Article 239AA,Article 294(b), Article 300,Article 359,Article 361,Article 372,Article 395;

Constitution of Ireland - Article 40, Constitution of Ireland - Article 40(3), Article 40(6);

Constitution of the Republic of South Africa, 1996 - Article 16(1), Article 16(2);

Convention on the Rights of Persons with Disabilities - Article 21; Convention on the Rights of the Child - Article 12, Convention on the Rights of the Child - Article 13;

Cable Television Networks (Regulation) Act, 1995; Crown Proceedings Act, 1947 - Section 3, Crown Proceedings Act, 1947 - Section 4, Crown

Proceedings Act, 1947 - Section 10; Disaster Management Act, 2005 - Section 12; East Punjab Public Safety Act, 1949 - Section 7(1); European Convention on Human Rights, 1950 - Article 10(1), European Convention on Human Rights, 1950 - Article 10(2); Guardians And Wards Act, 1890 - Section 19(b); Hindu Minority And Guardianship Act, 1956 - Section 6(a); Human Rights Act, 1998 - Article 10(1), Human Rights Act, 1998 - Article 10(2); Indian Criminal Law Amendment (Madras) Act, 1950; Indian Criminal Law Amendment Act, 1908 - Section 15(2); Indian Evidence Act, 1872 - Section 123;

Indian Penal Code, 1860 (IPC) -Section 107,Section 117,Section 124A,Section 144, Section 153A,Section 153B,Section 153A(1),Section 171C,Section 228, Section 228A,Section 292, Section 293, Section 295A, Section 298,Section 312, Section 342, Section 351, Section 354Section 354A,Section 354C,Section 354D, Section 355,Section 376, Section 376D, Section 383, Section 390, - Section 395,Section 397,Section 420, Section 493, Section 496, Section 498A, Section 499, Section 500, Section 504,Section 505,Section 505(1), Section 509,Section 354E;

Indian Stamp Act, 1899 - Section 73; Indian Telegraph Act, 1885 - Section 5(2); Information Technology Act, 2000 - Section 66A; International Covenant on Civil and Political Rights - Article 19, International Covenant on Civil and Political Rights - Article 19(3), International Covenant on Civil and Political Rights - Article 20; Judicial Officers' Protection Act, 1850 - Section 1; Madras Maintenance of Public Order Act, 1949 - Section 9(1A); Protection of Children from Sexual Offences Act, 2012; Protection Of Civil Rights Act, 1955 - Section 7; Religious Institutions (prevention Of Misuse) Act, 1988 - Section 3(g); Representation Of The People Act, 1951 - Section 8, Representation Of The People Act, 1951 - Section 123(3A), Representation Of The People Act, 1951 - Section 123(5), Representation of the People Act, 1951 - Section 124(5); Right Of Children To Free And Compulsory Education Act 2009 - Section 12; Right To Information Act, 2005 - Section 8(j), Right To Information Act, 2005 - Section 8(1); Scheduled Castes And The Scheduled Tribes (prevention Of Atrocities) Act, 1989 - Section 3(1); Protection of Human Rights Act, 1993; Prevention of Insults to National Honour Act, 1971; Code of Criminal Procedure (CrPC) Act, 1995; Racial Discrimination Act, 1975; Daily Newspaper (Price and Page) Order, 1960; Newspaper (Price and Page) Act, 1956; Civil Rights Act, 1875; Companies Act; Imports and Exports (Control) Act, 1947; Passports Act, 1967; Bonded Labour

System (Abolition) Act, 1976; Federal Tort Claims Act, 1946; Law Reform (Contributory Negligence) Act, 1945; Enemy Act, 1947; Manoeuvres, Field Firing and Artillery Practice Act, 1948; Seaward Artillery Practice Act, 1949; Indian Post Offices Act, 1898; Drugs and Magic Remedies (Objectionable Advertisements) Act, 1954; Specific Relief Act, 1963

Hon'ble Judges/Coram:

S. Abdul Nazeer, B.R. Gavai, A.S. Bopanna, V. Ramasubramanian and B.V. Nagarathna, JJ.

Equivalent Citation: 2023/INSC/4, (2023)4SCC1

Number of Pages in the Original Judgment:120

Case Reference:

Kasturilal Ralia Ram Jain v. State of Uttar Pradesh MANU/SC/0086/1964; Rudul Sah v. State of Bihar and Ors. MANU/SC/0380/1983; Nilabati Behera v. State of Orissa and Ors. MANU/SC/0307/1993; Thalappalam Ser. Coop. Bank Ltd. and Ors. v. State of Kerala and Ors. MANU/SC/1020/2013; R. Rajagopal and Ors. v. State of Tamil Nadu and Ors. MANU/SC/0056/1995; People's Union for civil Liberties (PUCL) and Ors. v. Union of India (UOI) and Ors. MANU/SC/0234/2003; Jumuna Prasad Mukhariya and Ors. v. Lachhi Ram and Ors. MANU/SC/0104/1954; Ram Jethmalani and Ors. v. Union of India (UOI) and Ors. MANU/SC/0711/2011; Sahara India Real Estate Corporation Ltd. and Ors. v. Securities and Exchange Board of India and Ors. MANU/SC/0735/2012; Subramanian Swamy v. Union of India (UOI) and Ors. MANU/SC/0621/2016; In Re: Noise Pollution - Implementation of the Laws for restricting use of loudspeakers and high volume producing sound systems MANU/SC/0415/2005; Asha Ranjan and Ors. v. State of Bihar and Ors. MANU/SC/0159/2017; People's Union for Democratic Rights and Ors. v. Union of India (UOI) and Ors. MANU/SC/0038/1982; M.C. Mehta v. Kamal Nath and Ors. MANU/SC/0416/2000; Justice K.S. Puttaswamy and Ors. v. Union of India (UOI) and Ors. MANU/SC/1044/2017; P.D. Shamdasani v. Central Bank of India Ltd. MANU/SC/0017/1951; State of West Bengal and Ors. v. The Committee for Protection of Democratic Rights, West Bengal and Ors. MANU/SC/0121/2010; S. Rangarajan and Ors. v. P. Jagjevan Ram and Ors. MANU/SC/0475/1989; Union of India (UOI) v. K. M. Shankarappa MANU/SC/0726/2000; Indibility Creative Pvt. Ltd. and Ors. v. Govt. of West Bengal and Ors. MANU/SC/0518/2019; Parmanand Katara v. Union of India (UOI) and Ors. MANU/SC/0423/1989; Amish Devgan v. Union of India (UOI) and Ors. MANU/SC/0921/2020; State of Maharashtra and Ors. v.

Sarangdharsingh Shivdassingh Chavan and Ors. MANU/SC/1055/2010; Secretary, Jaipur Development Authority, Jaipur v. Daulat Mal Jain and Ors. MANU/SC/1002/1997; Manoj Narula v. Union of India (UOI) MANU/SC/0736/2014; R. Sai Bharathi v. J. Jayalalitha and Ors. MANU/SC/0956/2003; Common Cause, A Registered Society v. Union of India (UOI) and Ors. MANU/SC/0437/1999; Sakal Papers (P) Ltd. and Ors. v. The Union of India (UOI) MANU/SC/0090/1961; The Praga Tools Corporation v. C.A. Imanual and Ors. MANU/SC/0327/1969; Anandi Mukta Sadguru Shree Muktajee Vandas Swami Suvarna Jayanti Mahotsav Smarak Trust and Ors. v. V.R. Rudani and Ors. MANU/SC/0028/1989; M.C. Mehta and Ors. v. Union of India (UOI) and Ors. MANU/SC/0092/1986; Binny Ltd. and Ors. v. V. Sadasivan and Ors. MANU/SC/0470/2005; Society for Un-aided Private Schools of Rajasthan v. Union of India (UOI) and Ors. MANU/SC/0311/2012; Pravasi Bhalai Sangathan v. Union of India (UOI) and Ors. MANU/SC/0197/2014; Kodungallur Film Society and Ors. v. Union of India (UOI) and Ors. MANU/SC/1107/2018; Romesh Thappar v. The State of Madras MANU/SC/0006/1950; Brij Bhushan and Ors. v. The State of Delhi MANU/SC/0007/1950; Express Newspapers (Private) Ltd. and Ors. v. The Union of India (UOI) and Ors. MANU/SC/0157/1958; Bijoe Emmanuel and Ors. v. State of Kerala and Ors. MANU/SC/0061/1986; Secretary, Ministry of Information and Broadcasting, Govt. of India and Ors. v. Cricket Association of Bengal and Ors. MANU/SC/0246/1995; Ramlila Maidan Incident v. Home Secretary, Union of India (UOI) and Ors. MANU/SC/0131/2012; Girish Ramchandra Deshpande v. Cen. Information Commr. and Ors. MANU/SC/0816/2012; Vikas Yadav v. State of U.P. and Ors. MANU/SC/1167/2016; Railway Board Representing The Union of India (UOI) v. Niranjan Singh MANU/SC/0507/1969; Life Insurance Corporation of India and Union of India (UOI) and Ors. v. Manubhai D. Shah and Cinemart Foundation MANU/SC/0032/1993; Vidya Verma, through next Friend R.V.S. Mani v. Shiv Narain Verma MANU/SC/0072/1955; Sukhdev Singh and Ors. v. Bhagat Ram and Ors. MANU/SC/0667/1975; Lucknow Development Authority v. M.K. Gupta MANU/SC/0178/1994; The Chairman, Railway Board and Ors. v. Chandrima Das and Ors. MANU/SC/0046/2000; M.C. Mehta v. Kamal Nath and Ors. MANU/SC/1007/1997; Vellore Citizens Welfare Forum v. Union of India (UOI) and Ors. MANU/SC/0686/1996; Indian Council for Enviro-Legal Action and Ors. v. Union of India (UOI) and Ors. MANU/SC/1112/1996; Consumer Education and Research center and Ors. v. Union of India (UOI) and Ors.

MANU/SC/0175/1995; Vishaka and Ors. v. State of Rajasthan and Ors. MANU/SC/0786/1997; Medha Kotwal Lele and Ors. v. Union of India (UOI) and Ors. MANU/SC/0898/2012; Githa Hariharan and Ors. v. Reserve Bank of India and Ors. MANU/SC/0117/1999; Indian Medical Association and Ors. v. Union of India (UOI) and Ors. MANU/SC/0608/2011; T.M.A. Pai Foundation and Ors. v. State of Karnataka and Ors. MANU/SC/0905/2002; Jeeja Ghosh and Ors. v. Union of India (UOI) and Ors. MANU/SC/0574/2016; Zee Telefilms Ltd. and Ors. v. Union of India (UOI) and Ors. MANU/SC/0074/2005; Janet Jeyapaul v. SRM University and Ors. MANU/SC/1438/2015; A.K. Gopalan v. The State of Madras MANU/SC/0012/1950; S. Krishnan and Ors. v. The State of Madras MANU/SC/0008/1951; Siddharam Satlingappa Mhetre v. State of Maharashtra and Ors. MANU/SC/1021/2010; Kharak Singh v. The State of U.P. and Ors. MANU/SC/0085/1962; Mohd. Arif and Ors. v. Registrar, Supreme Court of India and Ors. MANU/SC/0754/2014; Rustom Cavasjee Cooper and Ors. v. Union of India (UOI) MANU/SC/0011/1970; Govind v. State of Madhya Pradesh and Ors. MANU/SC/0119/1975; Satwant Singh Sawhney v. D. Ramarathnam and Ors. MANU/SC/0040/1967; Maneka Gandhi v. Union of India (UOI) and Ors. MANU/SC/0133/1978; Bandhua Mukti Morcha v. Union of India (UOI) and Ors. MANU/SC/0051/1983; National Human Rights Commission v. State of Arunachal Pradesh and Ors. MANU/SC/1047/1996; X' v. Hospital 'Z' MANU/SC/0733/1998; Suchita Srivastava and Ors. v. Chandigarh Administration MANU/SC/1580/2009; Devika Biswas v. Union of India (UOI) and Ors. MANU/SC/0999/2016; People's Union of Civil Liberties (PUCL) v. Union of India (UOI) and Ors. MANU/SC/0149/1997; Distt. Registrar and Collector, Hyderabad and Ors. v. Canara Bank and Ors. MANU/SC/0935/2004; In Re: Indian Woman says gang-raped on orders of Village Court published in Business and Financial News MANU/SC/0242/2014; Lata Singh v. State of U.P. and Ors. MANU/SC/2960/2006; Arumugam Servai v. State of Tamil Nadu MANU/SC/0434/2011; Shakti Vahini v. Union of India (UOI) and Ors. MANU/SC/0291/2018; A. Sanjeevi Naidu and Ors. v. State of Madras and Ors. MANU/SC/0381/1970; State of Karnataka v. Union of India (UOI) and Ors. MANU/SC/0144/1977; R.K. Jain v. Union of India (UOI) and Ors. MANU/SC/0291/1993; Vineet Narain and Ors. v. Union of India (UOI) and Ors. MANU/SC/0827/1998; Common Cause A Registered Society v. Union of India (UOI) and Ors. MANU/SC/0976/1996; Common Cause, A Regd. Society v. Union of India (UOI) and Ors. MANU/SC/1287/1996;

Government of NCT of Delhi v. Union of India (UOI) and Ors. MANU/SC/0680/2018; The State of Bihar v. Abdul Majid MANU/SC/0120/1954; The State of Rajasthan v. Vidhyawati and Ors. MANU/SC/0025/1962; Khatri and Ors. v. State of Bihar and Ors. MANU/SC/0518/1981; Sebastian M. Hongray v. Union of India (UOI) MANU/SC/0080/1984; Bhim Singh v. State of J and K and Ors. MANU/SC/0064/1985; Peoples' Union for Democratic Rights v. State of Bihar and Ors. MANU/SC/0104/1986; Saheli, A Women's Resources center, Through Ms Nalini Bhanot and Ors. v. Commissioner of Police Delhi Police Headquarters and Ors. MANU/SC/0478/1989; Supreme Court Legal Aid Committee v. State of Bihar and Ors. MANU/SC/0604/1991; Arvinder Singh Bagga v. State of U.P. and Ors. MANU/SC/0025/1995; N. Nagendra Rao and Co. v. State of Andhra Pradesh MANU/SC/0530/1994; Inder Singh v. State of Punjab and Ors. MANU/SC/0380/1995; Paschim Banga Khet Mazdoor Samity and Ors. v. State of West Bengal and Ors. MANU/SC/0611/1996; D.K. Basu v. State of West Bengal MANU/SC/0157/1997; People's Union for Civil Liberties v. Union of India (UOI) and Ors. MANU/SC/0274/1997; Municipal Corporation of Delhi, Delhi v. Association of Victims of Uphaar Tragedy and Ors. MANU/SC/1255/2011; S. Khushboo v. Kanniammal and Ors. MANU/SC/0310/2010; Shreya Singhal v. Union of India (UOI) MANU/SC/0329/2015; Kedar Nath Singh v. State of Bihar MANU/SC/0074/1962; Director General, Directorate General of Doordarshan and Ors. v. Anand Patwardhan and Ors. MANU/SC/3637/2006; Hamdard Dawakhana and Ors. v. Union of India (UOI) and Ors. MANU/SC/0016/1959; Indian Express Newspapers (Bombay) Private Ltd. and Ors. v. Union of India (UOI) and Ors. MANU/SC/0406/1984; Tata Press Ltd. v. Mahanagar Telephone Nigam Limited and Ors. MANU/SC/0745/1995; Union of India (UOI) and Ors. v. The Motion Picture Association and Ors. MANU/SC/0404/1999; National Legal Services Authority v. Union of India (UOI) and Ors. MANU/SC/0309/2014; Prabha Dutt v. Union of India (UOI) and Ors. MANU/SC/0087/1981; Swapnil Tripathi and Ors. v. Supreme Court of India and Ors. MANU/SC/1066/2018; Union of India (UOI) v. Naveen Jindal and Ors. MANU/SC/0072/2004; Charu Khurana v. Union of India (UOI) MANU/SC/1044/2014; Justice K.S. Puttaswamy and Ors. v. Union of India (UOI) and Ors. MANU/SC/1054/2018; Kesavananda Bharati Sripadagalvaru v. State of Kerala MANU/SC/0445/1973; Additional District Magistrate, Jabalpur v. Shivakant Shukla MANU/SC/0062/1976; Director of Rationing and Distribution v. The Corporation of Calcutta and

Ors. MANU/SC/0061/1960; People's Union for Civil Liberties v. Union of India (UOI) and Ors. MANU/SC/0039/2005; Zoroastrian Co-operative Housing Society Limited and Ors. v. District Registrar Co-operative Societies (Urban) and Ors. MANU/SC/0290/2005; Pradeep Kumar Biswas and Ors. v. Indian Institute of Chemical Biology and Ors. MANU/SC/0330/2002; Ramakrishna Mission and Ors. v. Kago Kunya and Ors. MANU/SC/0413/2019; Union of India (UOI) v. Paul Manickam and Ors. MANU/SC/0805/2003; Mohd. Ikram Hussain v. State of U.P. and Ors. MANU/SC/0241/1963; Nirmaljit Kaur v. State of Punjab and Ors. MANU/SC/2275/2005; Gaurav Kumar Bansal v. Union of India (UOI) MANU/SC/0790/2014; Swaraj Abhiyan - (I) v. Union of India (UOI) and Ors. MANU/SC/0553/2016; Peoples' Union For Democratic Rights Through Its Secretary and Ors. v. Police Commissioner, Delhi Police Headquarters and Ors. MANU/SC/0409/1989; State of Maharashtra and Ors. v. Ravikant S. Patil MANU/SC/0561/1991; Kumari v. State of Tamil Nadu and Ors. MANU/SC/0408/1992; Shakuntala Devi v. Delhi Electric Supply Undertaking and Ors. MANU/SC/0599/1995; Tamil Nadu Electricity Board v. Sumathi and Ors. MANU/SC/0338/2000; Hindustan Paper Corpn. Ltd. v. Ananta Bhattacharjee and Ors. MANU/SC/0654/2004; Delhi Jal Board v. National Campaign for Dignity and Rights of Sewerage and Allied Workers and Ors. MANU/SC/0794/2011; Ramana Dayaram Shetty v. International Airport Authority of India and Ors. MANU/SC/0048/1979; Bodhisattwa Gautam v. Subhra Chakraborty (Ms.) MANU/SC/0245/1996 : (1996) 1 SC 490; John Meskell v. Coras Iompair Eireann 1973 IR 121; Murtagh Properties Limited v. Cleary 1972 IR 330; Shelly v. Kraemer MANU/USSC/0145/1948 : 334 U.S. 1 (1948); Gitlow v. New York 286 US 652 (1925); State of Madras v. V.G. Row MANU/SC/0013/1952 : (1952) 1 SCC 410; Roth v. United States, MANU/USSC/0157/1957 : 354 U.S. 476 (1957); Ashcroft v. Free Speech Coalition, MANU/USSC/0029/2002 : 435 U.S. 234 (2002); Chaplinsky v. New Hampshire, MANU/USSC/0058/1942 : 315 U.S. 568 (1942); Virginia v. Black, MANU/USSC/0028/2003 : 538 U.S. 343 (2003); Jones v. Alfred H. Mayer Co MANU/USSC/0167/1968 : 392 US 409 (1968); New York Times v. Sullivan MANU/USSC/0245/1964 : 376 U.S. 254 (1964); Civil Rights Cases MANU/USSC/0280/1883 : 109 US 3 (1883); Du Plessis and Ors. v. De Klerk and Anr. MANU/SACC/0002/1996 : 1996 ZACC 10; Khumalo v. Holomisa MANU/SACC/0004/2002 : (2002) ZACC 12; Governing Body of the Juma Musjid Primary School and Ors. v. Essay N.O. and Ors. (CCT 29/10) MANU/SACC/0004/2011 : (2011) ZACC 13 : 2011 (8) BCLR 761

(CC); Douglas v. Hello! Ltd. MANU/UKWA/0302/2000 : (2001) QB 967; X v. Y (2004) EWCA Civ 662; ADT v. UK (2000) 2 FLR 697; "Arzte Fur Das Leben" v. Austria (1988) ECHR 15; X and Y v. The Netherlands (1985) ECHR 4; Marsh v. Alabama MANU/USSC/0102/1946 : 326 US 501 (1946); Merryweather v. Nixan MANU/ENRP/0635/1799 : (1799) 8 T.R. 186; Pravasi Bhalai Sangathan v. Union of India MANU/SC/0197/2014 : (2014) 11 SC 477; Saskatchewan Human Rights Commission v. William Whatcott, MANU/SCCN/0005/2013 : 2013 SCC 11; Chaplinsky v. State of New Hampshire MANU/USSC/0058/1942 : 315 U.S. 568 (1942); R v. James Keegstra (1990) 3 SCR 697; Canada Human Rights Commission v. Taylor MANU/SCCN/0071/1990 : (1990) 3 SCR 892; Pat Eatock v. Andrew Bolt (2011) FCA 1103; Peninsular & Oriental Steam Navigation Co. v. Secy. of State (1868-69) 5 Bom HCR APP 1; Luth Case (1958) BVerfGE 7, 198

Case Note:

V. Ramasubramanian, J. Constitution - Rights of a citizen - Writ petitions were dismissed by High Court, on the ground that the prayer of the public interest writ Petitioners were in the realm of moral values and that the question whether the Chief Minister should frame a code of conduct for the Ministers of his cabinet or not, is not within the domain of the Court to decide - Are the grounds specified in Article 19(2) in relation to which reasonable restrictions on the right to free speech can be imposed by law, exhaustive, or can restrictions on the right to free speech be imposed on grounds not found in Article 19(2) by invoking other fundamental rights - Can a fundamental right Under Article 19 or 21 of the Constitution of India be claimed other than against the 'State' or its instrumentalities - Whether the State is under a duty to affirmatively protect the rights of a citizen Under Article 21 of the Constitution of India even against a threat to the liberty of a citizen by the acts or omissions of another citizen or private agency - Can a statement made by a Minister, traceable to any affairs of State or for protecting the Government, be attributed vicariously to the Government itself, especially in view of the principle of Collective Responsibility - Whether a statement by a Minister, inconsistent with the rights of a citizen under Part Three of the Constitution, constitutes a violation of such constitutional rights and is actionable as 'Constitutional Tort"?

Facts:

Writ Petition (Criminal) No. 113 of 2016 was filed Under Article 32 of the Constitution praying for several reliefs including monitoring the investigation of a criminal complaint in FIR Under Section 154 Code of Criminal Procedure, for the offences Under Sections 395, 397 and 376-D read with the relevant provisions of the Protection of Children from Sexual Offences Act, 2012 ('POCSO Act') and for the trial of the case outside the State and also for registering a complaint against the then Minister for Urban Development of the Government of U.P. for making statements outrageous to the modesty of the victims. Insofar as Special Leave Petition (Diary) No. 34629 of 2017 is concerned, the same arose out of a judgment of the Division Bench of the Kerala High Court dismissing two writ petitions. The writ petitions were filed in public interest on the ground that the then Minister for Electricity in the State of Kerala issued certain statements in February 2016, 7.4.2017 and 22.4.2017. These statements were highly derogatory of women. Though according to the Petitioners in the public interest litigation, the political party to which the Minister belonged, issued a public censure, no action was taken officially against the Minister. Therefore, the Petitioner in one writ petition prayed among other things for a direction to the Chief Minister to frame a Code of Conduct for the Ministers who have subscribed to the oath of office as prescribed by the Constitution with a further direction to the Chief Minister to take suitable action if any of the Ministers failed to live upto the oath. The prayer in the second writ petition was for a direction to the concerned Authorities to take action against the Minister for his utterances. Both the writ petitions were dismissed by a Division Bench of the Kerala High Court, on the ground that the prayer of the public interest writ Petitioners were in the realm of moral values and that the question whether the Chief Minister should frame a code of conduct for the Ministers of his cabinet or not, is not within the domain of the Court to decide.

Held, while answering the reference

1.The grounds lined up in Article 19(2) for restricting the right to free speech are exhaustive. Under the guise of invoking other fundamental rights or under the guise of two fundamental rights staking a competing claim against each other, additional restrictions not found in Article 19(2), cannot be imposed on the exercise of the right conferred by Article 19(1)(a) upon any individual. A fundamental right Under Article 19/21 can be enforced even against persons other than the State or its instrumentalities. The State is under a duty to affirmatively protect the rights of a person Under Article 21, whenever there is a threat to personal liberty, even by a non-State actor. A statement made by a Minister even if traceable to any affairs of the State or for protecting the Government, cannot be attributed vicariously to the Government by invoking the principle of collective responsibility. A mere statement made by a Minister, inconsistent with the rights of a citizen under Part-III of the Constitution, may not constitute a violation of the constitutional rights and become actionable as Constitutional tort. But if as a consequence of such a statement, any act of omission or commission is done by the officers resulting in harm or loss to a person/citizen, then the same may be actionable as a constitutional tort. [155]

B.V. Nagarathna, J.

2.The rights in the realm of common law, which may be similar or identical in their content to the Fundamental Rights Under Article 19/ 21, operate horizontally: However, the Fundamental Rights Under Articles 19 and 21, may not be justiciable horizontally before the Constitutional Courts except those rights which have been statutorily recognised and in accordance with the applicable law. However, they may be the basis for seeking common law remedies. But a remedy in the form of writ of Habeas Corpus, if sought against a private person on the basis of Article 21 of the Constitution can be before a Constitutional Court i.e., by way of Article 226 before the High Court or Article 32 read with Article 142 before the Supreme Court. [199]

3.The duty cast upon the State Under Article 21 is a negative duty not to deprive a person of his life and personal liberty except in accordance with law. The State has an affirmative duty to carry out obligations cast upon it under statutory and constitutional law, which are based on the Fundamental Right guaranteed Under Article 21 of the Constitution. Such obligations may require interference by the State where acts of a private actor may threaten the life or liberty of another individual. Failure to carry out the duties enjoined upon the State under statutory law to protect the rights of a citizen, could have the effect of depriving a citizen of his right to life and personal liberty. When a citizen is so deprived of his right to life and personal liberties, the State would have breached the negative duty cast upon it Under Article 21. [200]

4. A Minster may make statements in two capacities: first, in his personal capacity; second, in his official capacity and as a delegate of the Government. It is a no brainer that in respect of the former category of statements, no vicarious liability may be attributed to the Government itself. The latter category of statements may be traceable to any affair of the State or may be made with a view to protect the Government. If such

statements are disparaging or derogatory and represent not only the personal views of the individual Minister making them, but also embody the views of the Government, then, such statements can be attributed vicariously to the Government itself, especially in view of the principle of Collective Responsibility. In other words, if such views are endorsed not only in the statements made by an individual Minister, but are also reflective of the Government's stance, such statements may be attributed vicariously to the Government. However, if such statements are stray opinions of an individual Minister and are not consistent with the views of the Government, then they shall be attributable to the Minister personally and not to the Government. A statement made by a Minister if traceable to any affairs of the State or for protecting the Government, can be attributed vicariously to the Government by invoking the principle of collective responsibility, so long as such statement represents the view of the Government also. If such a statement is not consistent with the view of the Government, then it is attributable to the Minister personally. [201]

5. While it is true that the Courts must mould their tools to deal with particularly extreme and threatening situations, and the device of a 'constitutional tort' has evolved through such an exercise, it must be borne in mind that the tool of treating an action as a constitutional tort must not be wielded only in instances wherein state lawlessness and indifference to the right to life and personal liberties have caused immense suffering. The law would have to evolve in this regard, in respect of violation of other Fundamental Rights apart from issuance of the prerogative writs. [221]

6. Therefore, it is observed that presently invocation of writ jurisdiction to grant damages, by treating acts and omissions of agencies of the State as Constitutional torts, must be an exception rather than a rule. The remedy before a competent court or under criminal law is, in any case available as per the existing legal framework. A proper legal framework is necessary to define the acts or omissions which would amount to constitutional tort and the manner in which the same would be redressed or remedied on the basis of judicial precedent. [222]

7.It is for the Parliament in its wisdom to enact a legislation or code to restrain, citizens in general and public functionaries, in particular, from making disparaging or vitriolic remarks against fellow citizens, having regard to the strict parameters of Article 19(2) and bearing in mind the freedom Under Article 19(1) (a) of the Constitution of India. It is also for the respective political parties to regulate and control the actions and speech of its functionaries and members. This could be through enactment of a Code of Conduct which would prescribe the limits of permissible speech by functionaries and members of the respective political parties. Any citizen, who is prejudiced by any form of attack, as a result of speech/ expression through any medium, targeted against her/him or by speech which constitutes 'hate speech' or any species thereof, whether such attack or speech is by a public functionary or otherwise, may approach the Court of Law under Criminal and Civil statutes and seek appropriate remedies. Whenever permissible, civil remedies in the nature of declaratory remedies, injunctions as well as pecuniary damages may be awarded as prescribed under the relevant statutes. [223]

Ratio Decidendi:

A mere statement made by a Minister, inconsistent with the rights of a citizen under Part-III of the Constitution, may not constitute a violation of the constitutional rights.

• • •

CHAPTER XVIII

Usha Chakraborty and Ors. vs. State of West Bengal and Ors. (30.01.2023 – SC) : MANU/SC/0079/2023

Relative Section:

Code of Criminal Procedure, 1973 (CrPC) - Section 156 (3), Code of Criminal Procedure, 1973 (CrPC) - Section 155(2), Code of Criminal Procedure, 1973 (CrPC) - Section 156(1), Code of Criminal Procedure, 1973 (CrPC) - Section 156(3), Code of Criminal Procedure, 1973 (CrPC) - Section 482; Indian Penal Code, 1860 (IPC) - Section 120B, Indian Penal Code, 1860 (IPC) - Section 323, Indian Penal Code, 1860 (IPC) - Section 334, Indian Penal Code, 1860 (IPC) - Section 384, Indian Penal Code, 1860 (IPC) - Section 406, Indian Penal Code, 1860 (IPC) - Section 420, Indian Penal Code, 1860 (IPC) - Section 423, Indian Penal Code, 1860 (IPC) - Section 466, Indian Penal Code, 1860 (IPC) - Section 467, Indian Penal Code, 1860 (IPC) - Section 468

Hon'ble Judges/Coram: Ajay Rastogi and C.T. Ravikumar, JJ.

Equivalent Citation: 2023(244)AIC184, AIR2023SC688, 2023 (1) ALT (Crl.) 238 (A.P.), 2023(1)Crimes308(SC), 2023/INSC/86, 2023(1)UC531

Number of Pages in the Original Judgment: 13

Case Reference:

Paramjeet Batra v. State of Uttarakhand and Ors. MANU/SC/1108/2012; Vesa Holdings P. Ltd. and Ors. v. State of Kerala and Ors. MANU/SC/0298/2015; Kapil Agarwal and Ors. v. Sanjay Sharma and Ors. MANU/SC/0131/2021; State of Haryana and Ors. v. Ch. Bhajan Lal and Ors. MANU/SC/0115/1992; Neeharika Infrastructure Pvt. Ltd. v. State of Maharashtra and Ors. MANU/SC/0272/2021

Case Note:

Criminal - Quashing of proceedings - Sections 120B, 323, 384, 406, 420, 423, 467 and 468 of Indian Penal Code, 1860 - Appellants approached High Court seeking quashing of F.I.R. registered against them and two others under Sections 323, 384, 406, 423, 467, 468, 420 and 120B of Code - High Court declined to exercise jurisdiction holding that perusal of case diary as also materials appearing therefrom prima facie made out case for investigation - Hence, present appeal - Whether proceedings initiated against Appellants for alleged offences liable to quashed.

Facts:

An F.I.R. registered against them and two others under Sections 323, 384, 406, 423, 467, 468, 420 and 120B of Indian Penal Code, 1860. The Appellants approached the High Court seeking quashment of F.I.R. registered against them and two others, under Sections 323, 384, 406, 423, 467, 468, 420 and 120B of Indian Penal Code (I.P.C.) raising various grounds. The High Court declined to exercise the jurisdiction holding that perusal of the case diary as also the materials appearing therefrom prima facie made out a case for investigation.

Held, while allowing the appeal:

(i) The materials on record pertaining to the said pleadings instituted in the Civil Suit, produced in this proceeding would reveal that the Respondent was in fact ousted from the membership of the trust. In the counter affidavit filed in this proceeding, the Respondent had virtually admitted the pendency of the suit filed against his removal from the post of Secretary and the trusteeship and its pendency. The factum of passing of adverse orders in the interlocutory applications in the said Civil Suit as also the prima facie finding and conclusion arrived at by the Civil Court that the Respondent stands removed from the post of Secretary and also from the trusteeship are also not disputed therein. Then, the question was why would the Respondent conceal those relevant aspects. The indisputable and undisputed facts would reveal the existence of the civil dispute on removal of the Respondent from the post of Secretary of the school as also from the trusteeship. Obviously, it could only be taken that since the removal from the office of the Secretary and the trusteeship was the causative incident, he concealed the pendency of the civil suit to cover up the civil nature of the dispute. [9]

(ii) By non-disclosure the Respondent has, in troth, concealed the existence of a pending civil suit between him and the Appellants herein before a competent civil court which obviously was the causative incident for the Respondent's allegation of perpetration of the aforesaid offences against the Appellants. There could not be any doubt with respect to the position that in order to cause registration of an F.I.R. and consequential investigation based on the same the petition filed under Code of Criminal Procedure, must satisfy the essential ingredients to attract the alleged offences. In other words, if such allegations in the petition were vague and were not specific with respect to the alleged offences it could not lead to an order for registration of an F.I.R. and investigation on the accusation of commission of the offences alleged. As noticed hereinbefore, the Respondent alleged commission of offences under Sections 323, 384, 406, 423, 467, 468, 420 and 120B, Indian Penal Code against the Appellants. A bare perusal of the said allegation and the ingredients to attract them, would reveal that the allegations were vague and they did not carry the essential ingredients to constitute the alleged offences. There was absolutely no allegation in the complaint that the Appellants had caused hurt on the Respondent so also, they did not reveal a case that the Appellants had intentionally put the Respondent in fear of injury either to himself or another or by putting him under such fear or injury, dishonestly induced him to deliver any property or valuable security. The same was the position with respect to the alleged offences punishable Under Sections 406, 423, 467, 468, 420 and 120B, Indian Penal Code. The ingredients to attract the alleged offence referred to hereinbefore and the nature of the allegations contained in the application filed by the Respondent would undoubtedly make it clear that the Respondent had failed to make specific allegation against the Appellants herein in respect of the aforesaid offences. The factual position thus would reveal that the genesis as also the purpose of criminal proceedings were nothing but the aforesaid incident and further that the dispute involved was essentially of civil nature. The Appellants and the Respondents had given a cloak of criminal offence in the issue. In such circumstance when the Respondent had already resorted to the available civil remedy and it was pending, going by the decision in Paramjit Batra, the High Court would have quashed the criminal proceedings to prevent the abuse of the process of the Court but for the concealment. [10]

Disposition: In Favour of Accused.

• • •

CHAPTER XIX

Ramesh Chandra Gupta vs. State of U.P. and Ors. (28.11.2022 – SC) : MANU/SC/1551/2022

Relative Section:

Code of Criminal Procedure, 1973 (CrPC) - Section 155(2), Code of Criminal Procedure, 1973 (CrPC) - Section 156(1), Code of Criminal Procedure, 1973 (CrPC) - Section 156(3), Code of Criminal Procedure, 1973 (CrPC) - Section 482; Constitution of India - Article 226; Indian Penal Code, 1860 (IPC) - Section 386, Indian Penal Code, 1860 (IPC) - Section 387, Indian Penal Code, 1860 (IPC) - Section 420, Indian Penal Code, 1860 (IPC) - Section 447, Indian Penal Code, 1860 (IPC) - Section 448, Indian Penal Code, 1860 (IPC) - Section 467, Indian Penal Code, 1860 (IPC) - Section 468, Indian Penal Code, 1860 (IPC) - Section 471, Indian Penal Code, 1860 (IPC) - Section 504, Indian Penal Code, 1860 (IPC) - Section 506

Hon'ble Judges/Coram: Ajay Rastogi and C.T. Ravikumar, JJ.

Equivalent Citation: 2023(2)ACR2037, 2023(241)AIC19, 2023 (122) ACC 669, (2023)1CALLT225(SC), 134(2022)CLT961, 2022(4)Crimes573(SC), 2023(1)CriminalCC229, 2022/INSC/1233, 2022 (7) KHC 556, 2023(1)RCR(Criminal)498

Number of Pages in the Original Judgment: 9

Case Reference:

Vineet Kumar and Ors. v. State of U.P. and Ors. MANU/SC/0351/2017; State of Karnataka v. L. Muniswamy and Ors. MANU/SC/0143/1977; State of Haryana and Ors. v. Ch. Bhajan Lal and Ors. MANU/SC/0115/1992; Neeharika Infrastructure Pvt. Ltd. v. State of Maharashtra and Ors. MANU/SC/0272/2021

Case Note:

Criminal - Quashing of proceedings - Section 482 of Code of Criminal Procedure, 1973 (CrPC) - Instant appeals have been filed against the judgment passed by the High Court dismissing the criminal miscellaneous application filed at the instance of the present Appellants - Whether High Court ought to have exercised its jurisdiction for quashing the entire criminal proceedings?

Facts:

The dispute relates to House No. 189, Mohalla Madia, Kanpur Road, Jhansi, which as per the complainant, was purchased in the name of Shravan Kumar Gupta, who was minor at that time, by means of a registered sale deed dated 4th May, 1977 and through the ostensible owner, the de-facto complainant purchased the property by registered sale deed dated 22nd December, 2018, but prior thereto, a family settlement took place in the family comprising of Ram Kumari, widow of Raja Ram Gupta and her four sons, namely, Ramesh Chandra Gupta, Ashok Kumar, Shravan Kumar and Vinod Kumar and a Memorandum of Understanding (MOU) was executed between the parties on 19th August, 2006 and in terms of the aforesaid MOU, the house came in the share of Vinod Kumar Gupta and while the Original Suit filed at the instance of Vinod Kumar Gupta was pending adjudication, the ostensible owner Shravan Kumar Gupta executed a registered sale deed dated 22nd December, 2018 in favour of the de-facto complainant and according to the informant/second Respondent, who is the vendee of the aforementioned registered sale deed, possession by title in favour of Shravan Kumar Gupta over the house in dispute came to be transferred in his favour and possession of the same was also handed over to him (de-facto complainant). The de-facto complainant/second Respondent, Atul Shukla, had a grievance that he was dispossessed from the subject property in question in reference to which a complaint was made Under Section 156(3) Code of Criminal Procedure with the concerned Magistrate. As a consequence of the aforesaid, an FIR came to be registered as Case Crime u der Sections 420, 467, 468, 471, 504, 506, 447, 386 of Indian Penal Code, P.S. Navabad, District Jhansi. Learned Counsel for the Appellants submits that the present is a case where the High Court ought to have exercised its jurisdiction for quashing the entire criminal proceedings. The criminal proceedings against the present Appellants were nothing but to put pressure on the Appellants and to harass them.

Held, while allowing the appeal

1. The pith and substance of the complaint of the de-facto complainant/ second Respondent is that the subject property was sold by the ostensible owner, Shravan Kumar Gupta, in reference to which registered sale deed was executed in his favour on 22nd Dec., 2018, but he was later dispossessed from the subject property. [11]

2. Subsequent to the aforesaid FIR, the investigating officer conducted investigation and later submitted a charge-sheet dated 24th June, 2019,

whereby named Accused i.e. the Appellants herein have been charge-sheeted Under Sections 420, 467, 468, 471, 504, 506, 448, 387 of IPC. Upon submission of the charge-sheet, the learned CJM, Jhansi, by an order dated 13th August, 2019 took cognizance and summoned the present Accused Appellants. [12]

3. Being aggrieved by the aforesaid, the Appellants who were charge-sheeted, approached the High Court by filing a Miscellaneous Application Under Section 482 of CrPC.That came to be dismissed by the High Court under the judgment impugned which is the subject matter of challenge in appeals. [13]

4. The High Court under the impugned judgment has even failed to examine as to what was the complaint and how the present Appellants are, in any manner, concerned with the so-called alleged commission of crime, but after recording superficial observations regarding the scope of interference Under Section 482 of CrPC dismissed the petition under the order impugned. [14]

5. The present case is fully covered by categories (1) and (3), as enumerated in State of Haryana and Ors. v. Bhajan Lal and Ors. A bare perusal of the complaint on the basis of which FIR came to be registered at the instance of the de-facto complainant/second Respondent does not disclose any act of the present Appellants or their participation in the commission of crime. They are neither concerned with the registered sale deed dated 4th May, 1977 nor the later sale deed executed in favour of the de-facto complainant by Shravan Kumar Gupta dated 22nd December, 2018, nor in possession of the subject property nor are parties to the civil proceedings and it is not the case of the complainant that either the Appellants have played any active/passive role either in scribing the document or are facilitators or witness to the document in reference to which the complaint has been made for cheating and committing forgery or have played any role in delivery of possession of the subject property in question. [18]

6. The de-facto complainant has implicated the present Appellants being members of the family to put pressure for obtaining possession of the subject property and to settle the civil dispute which is pending between Vinod Kumar Gupta, Shravan Kumar Gupta and the de-facto complainant in Original Suit. [19]

7. In the present facts and circumstances, the High Court ought to have exercised its power under Section 482 of CrPC for quashing of the

criminal complaint and proceedings in consequence thereof qua the present Appellants. [20]

8. The judgment impugned of the High Court is set aside and FIR and all the consequential proceedings qua the present Appellants stand quashed. Appeals allowed. [23]

Disposition: In Favour of Accused.

• • •

CHAPTER XX

The State of Maharashtra and Ors. vs. Maroti (02.11.2022 – SC) : MANU/SC/1420/2022

Relative Section:

Code of Criminal Procedure, 1973 (CrPC) - Section 53A,Section 155(2),Section 156(1),Section 161,Section 164, Section 164A,Section 173(2),Section 482;

Constitution of India - Article 15, Article 39(f);

United Nations Convention on Rights of Children - Article 3(2), Article 34;

Indian Evidence Act,1872 -Section 59,Section 145, Section 157;

Indian Penal Code, 1860 (IPC) - Section 26,Section 34,Section 376AB, Section 420, Section 471;

Maharashtra Prevention And Eradication Of Human Sacrifice And Other Inhuman, Evil And Aghori Practices And Black Magic Act, 2013 - Section 3;

Protection Of Children From Sexual Offences Act, 2012 - Section 4, Section 6,Section 19,Section 19(1), - Section 19(2),Section 20,Section 21,Section 21(1),Section 21(2), Section 27(1);

Protection of Women from Domestic Violence Act, 2005;

Scheduled Castes And The Scheduled Tribes (prevention Of Atrocities) Act, 1989 - Section 3(1), Scheduled Castes And The Scheduled Tribes (prevention Of Atrocities) Act, 1989 - Section 3(2)

Hon'ble Judges/Coram:

Ajay Rastogi and C.T. Ravikumar, JJ.

Equivalent Citation:

2023(242)AIC195, AIR2022SC5595, 2023 (123) ACC 286, 2022ALLMR(Cri)4597, 2023 (1) ALT (Crl.) 5 (A.P.), 2022(6)BLJ203, 2022(4)BomCR(Cri)316, 2023CriLJ818, 2022/INSC/1152, 2022(4)J.L.J.R.434, 2022(4)PLJR313, 2022(4)RCR(Criminal)934, (2023)4SCC298, 2023(2)UC980

Number of Pages in the Original Judgment: 10

Case Reference:

Shalu Ojha v. Prashant Ojha MANU/SC/0835/2014; R.P. Kapur v. The State of Punjab MANU/SC/0086/1960; State of Haryana and Ors. v. Ch.

Bhajan Lal and Ors. MANU/SC/0115/1992; State of Madhya Pradesh v. Awadh Kishore Gupta and Ors. MANU/SC/0946/2003; Monica Kumar and Ors. v. State of U.P. and Ors. MANU/SC/7760/2008; Shiji and Ors. v. Radhika and Ors. MANU/SC/1341/2011; Shankar Kisanrao Khade v. State of Maharashtra MANU/SC/0476/2013; M.L. Bhatt v. M.K. Pandita and Ors. MANU/SC/0340/2002; Rajeev Kourav v. Baisahab and Ors. MANU/SC/0163/2020; Vijay Madanlal Choudhary and Ors. v. Union of India and Ors. MANU/SC/0924/2022; A.S. Krishnan and Ors. v. State of Kerala MANU/SC/0233/2004

Case Note:

Criminal - Quashing of FIR - Sections 161, 164 and 482 of Code of Criminal Procedure, 1973 (CrPC) - High Court passed the impugned judgment and quashed the FIR as also the chargesheet qua the Respondent, Hence, present appeal - Whether impugned judgment resulting in quashment of the stated FIR and the charge-sheet is sustainable?

Facts:

Apprehending arrest in connection for the offences under Section 376AB of the Indian Penal Code, 1860, Section 4 and 6 of POCSO Act, Section 3(1)(w) and 3(2)(v) of the Scheduled Castes and Scheduled Tribes (Prevention of Atrocities) Act, 1989 and Section 3 of the Maharashtra Prevention and Eradication of Human Sacrifice and other Inhuman, Evil and Aghori Practices and Black Magic Act, 2013 said crime, the Respondent herein filed an anticipatory bail application before the Ld. Sessions Judge and the same was rejected. The said order was challenged before the High Court and the High Court allowed the appeal and granted him protection from arrest. Thereafter, the Respondent herein filed Criminal Application under Section 482 of the Code of Criminal Procedure seeking quashment of the FIR and the chargesheet to the extent they are against him. The High Court passed the impugned judgment and quashed the FIR as also the chargesheet qua the Respondent. Hence, this appeal.

Held, while allowing the appeal

1. The FIR registered in the case on hand would reveal that it came to be registered on coming to know about the suspected commission of sexual offence against minor tribal girl(s) against unidentified person(s). Failure to report regarding the commission of the offence under the POCSO Act despite knowledge about the same is the accusation against the Respondent revealed from the charge-sheet. The FIR reveals the ingredients of an offence under the POCSO Act and the real magnitude of the same was

revealed during the investigation, as stated above. On completion of the investigation, based on the materials collected, the Officer-in-Charge of the police station concerned formed an opinion that a cognizable offence as mentioned therein, appears to had been committed and that the persons named therein, including the Respondent herein, appears to have committed the offences specified against them and filed final report under Section 173(2) for prosecuting them. It is the stated FIR dated 12.04.2019 and the stated chargesheet dated 08.06.2019 which were sought to be quashed and consequently quashed as per the impugned judgment. [17]

2. If FIR and the materials collected disclose a cognizable offence and the final report filed Under Section 173(2) of CrPC on completion of investigation based on it would reveal that the ingredients to constitute an offence under the POCSO Act and a prima facie case against the persons named therein as Accused, the truthfulness, sufficiency or admissibility of the evidence are not matters falling within the purview of exercise of power Under Section 482 of CrPC and undoubtedly they are matters to be done by the Trial Court at the time of trial. [18]

3. There can be no dispute with respect to the position that statements recorded Under Section 161 of CrPC are inadmissible in evidence and its use is limited for the purposes as provided under Sections 145 and 157 of the Indian Evidence Act, 1872. As a matter of fact, statement recorded under Section 164 of CrPC can also be used only for such purposes. [20]

4. In the instant case, a scanning of the recitals in paragraph No. 10 of the impugned judgment would undoubtedly reveal the fact that the High Court had formed an opinion on perusal of the statement of a teacher of the victims and also the statements of the victims that sexual assault was detected only from the General Hospital, Chandrapur and then arrived at the conclusion that the Respondent was not made aware of sexual assault committed on the victims and there is no evidence to implicate him in the said crime. [21]

5. Thus, a bare perusal of the above extracted recitals from paragraph No. 10 of the impugned judgment would reveal that the High Court had gone through the statements of victims/witnesses cited by the prosecution, to arrive at the conclusion as to the existence or otherwise of evidence against the Respondent. Statements recorded Under Section 161 of CrPC are inadmissible in evidence and, therefore, could not have been made the basis for arriving at such conclusions. The FIR carries suspicion of commission of sexual assault and the charge-sheet reveals prima facie

against the Respondent in relation to non-reporting of such an offence under the POCSO Act. The very case of the Appellant is that some among the seventeen victims have given statements Under Section 161, Code of Criminal Procedure and some others Under Section 164 Code of Criminal Procedure, specifically stating that the Respondent was informed of the sexual assault on them. When that be the position, the High Court should not have embarked upon an enquiry, especially by looking into the statements of the victims recorded as also their teacher to form an opinion regarding the availability of evidence to connect the Respondent with the crime. [22]

6. High Court was not justified in bringing abrupt termination of the proceedings qua the Respondent. There is prima facie case against the Respondent for the offence referred above. [24]

7. The impugned judgment resulting in quashment of the stated FIR and the charge-sheet throttling the prosecution at the threshold, without allowing the materials in support of it to see the light of the day, cannot be said to be as an exercise done to secure interests of justice whereas it can only be stated that such exercise resulted in miscarriage of justice. [25]

8. The impugned judgment of the High Court is set aside and the Appeal is, accordingly allowed. [26]

Disposition: In Favour of State.

• • •

CHAPTER XXI

Jigar vs. State of Gujarat (23.09.2022 – SC) : MANU/SC/1233/2022

Relative Section:

Code of Criminal Procedure, 1973 (CrPC) - Section 2, Section 57,Section 167,Section 167(1),Section 167(2), Section 209,Section 438,Section 460,Section 461,Section 465(2),Section 482;

Constitution of India - Article 14, Article 21;

Gujarat Control Of Terrorism And Organised Crime Act, 2015 - Section 3(1), Gujarat Control Of Terrorism And Organised Crime Act, 2015 - Section 3(2), Gujarat Control Of Terrorism And Organised Crime Act, 2015 - Section 3(3), Gujarat Control Of Terrorism And Organised Crime Act, 2015 - Section 3(4), Gujarat Control Of Terrorism And Organised Crime Act, 2015 - Section 3(5), Gujarat Control Of Terrorism And Organised Crime Act, 2015 - Section 4, Gujarat Control Of Terrorism And Organised Crime Act, 2015 - Section 20, Gujarat Control Of Terrorism And Organised Crime Act, 2015 - Section 20(2), Gujarat Control Of Terrorism And Organised Crime Act, 2015 - Section 20(4), Gujarat Control Of Terrorism And Organised Crime Act, 2015 - Section 20(5); Maharashtra Control Of Organised Crime Act, 1999 - Section 21(5); Prevention Of Terrorism Act, 2002 - Section 49(2); Terrorist And Disruptive Activities (prevention) Act, 1987 - Section 20(4); Narcotic Drugs and Psychotropic Substances Act, 1985

Hon'ble Judges/Coram: Ajay Rastogi and Abhay Shreeniwas Oka, JJ.

Equivalent Citation: 2022(240)AIC206, AIR2022SC4641, 2023 (122) ACC 349, 2022(6)BLJ301, 134(2022)CLT608, 2022(4)Crimes10(SC), 2022/INSC/1013, (2023)6SCC484

Number of Pages in the Original Judgment: 22

Case Reference:

Hitendra Vishnu Thakur and Ors. v. State of Maharashtra and Ors. MANU/SC/0526/1994; Sanjay Dutt v. State through C.B.I., Bombay MANU/SC/0554/1994; Ateef Nasir Mulla v. State of Maharashtra MANU/SC/0507/2005; Sanjay Kumar Kedia v. Intelligence Officer, Narcotic Control Bureau and Ors. MANU/SC/1963/2009; S. Kasi v. State MANU/

SC/0491/2020; Bikramjit Singh v. The State of Punjab MANU/SC/0749/2020; M. Ravindran v. The Intelligence Officer, Directorate of Revenue Intelligence MANU/SC/0788/2020; Muzammil Pasha and Ors. v. National Investigating Agency and Ors. MANU/KA/2332/2021; Narendra G. Goel v. State of Maharashtra and Ors. MANU/SC/0885/2009; The State of Maharashtra v. Surendra Pundlik Gadling and Ors. MANU/SC/0195/2019; State of Maharashtra v. Bharat Shanti Lal Shah and Ors. MANU/SC/3789/2008; Fertico Marketing and Investment Pvt. Ltd. and Ors. v. Central Bureau of Investigation and Ors. MANU/SC/0864/2020; Securities and Exchange Board of India and Ors. v. Gaurav Varshney and Ors. MANU/SC/0778/2016; Uday Mohanlal Acharya v. State of Maharashtra MANU/SC/0222/2001; Mohamed Iqbal Madar Sheikh and Ors. v. State of Maharashtra MANU/SC/1045/1996; Rakesh Kumar Paul v. State of Assam MANU/SC/0993/2017; Devinderpal Singh v. Govt. of National Capital Territory of Delhi MANU/SC/1011/1996; Bharat Shanti Lal Shah and Ors. v. State of Maharashtra MANU/MH/0142/2003 : 2003 All Mr. (Crl.) 1061

Case Note:

Criminal - Investigation - Section 167 of Code of Criminal Procedure, 1973 (CrPC) - Challenge in present case is to an order granting extension to complete investigation - Whether orders granting extension to complete investigation are illegal?

Facts:

Appellants are the Accused in FIR registered with Jamnagar City 'A' Division Police Station in Gujarat for the offences Under Sections 3(1), 3(2), 3(3), 3(4), 3(5), and 4 of The Gujarat Control of Terrorism and Organised Crime Act, 2015 ('the 2015 Act'). The aforesaid First Information Report was registered on 15th October 2020. The Accused were arrested on different dates. Reports were submitted by the Public Prosecutor seeking extension of time up to 180 days to complete the investigation. In three cases, the reports were submitted on 8th January 2021, and in one case, it was submitted on 21st January 2021. The prayer for extending the time up to 180 days was allowed by the Special Court on the very day on which the applications were filed. Being aggrieved by the said orders of the Special Court, separate applications Under Section 482 of CrPC were preferred by the Appellants. By the impugned common Judgment, the learned Single Judge of Gujarat High Court rejected the applications made by the Appellants Under Section 482 of CrPC.

Held, while allowing the appeal

1. In the facts of the cases in hand, when the Special Court considered the reports submitted by the Public Prosecutor for grant of extension of time, the presence of the Appellants was admittedly not procured before the Special Court either personally or through video conference. It is also an admitted position that information about the filing of such reports by the Public Prosecutor was not provided to the Accused. It is mentioned in the impugned judgment that due to COVID - 19, it was not permissible to physically produce the Accused before the Special Court. Moreover, the Accused were in different prisons and, therefore, the production through video conference would have been very slow. Assuming that the process of production would have been slow, that is no excuse for not procuring the presence of the Accused through video conference. Nothing is placed on record either before this Court or High Court to show that as per the Standard Operating Procedure applicable to the concerned Court in January 2021 when the impugned orders were passed granting the extension, it was not permissible to physically produce the Accused before the Special Court. There is no material placed on record to show that technical reasons/difficulties prevented the prosecution from producing the Accused before the Special Court through video conference. It is not possible to accept that in January 2021 in the Court at Rajkot in the State of Gujarat, there was any connectivity issue. In fact, admittedly, no such case was pleaded before the High Court in the pleadings of the Respondents. [33]

2. The reports were submitted by the Public Prosecutor nearly a week before the expiry of the period of 90 days. In every case, period of seven days or more was available for completion of the period of ninety days. The orders were passed by the Special Court on the reports of the Public Prosecutor on the very day on which reports were submitted. There was no reason for such hurry. The Special Court could have always granted time of a couple of days to the prosecution to procure the presence of the Accused either physically or through video conference. The Accused may not be entitled to know the contents of the report but he is entitled to oppose the grant of extension of time on the grounds available to him in law. In the facts of the present case, the grant of extension of time without complying with the requirements laid down by the Constitution Bench has deprived the Accused of their right to seek default bail. It has resulted in the failure of justice. [34]

3. The orders passed by the Special Court of extending the period of investigation are rendered illegal on account of the failure of the

Respondents to produce the Accused before the Special Court either physically or virtually when the prayer for grant of extension made by the Public Prosecutor was considered. It was the duty of the Special Court to ensure that this important procedural safeguard was followed. Moreover, the oral notice, as contemplated by this Court in the case of Sanjay Dutt , was also not given to the Accused. [35]

4. Once it is held that the orders granting extension to complete investigation are illegal and stand vitiated, it follows that the Appellants are entitled to default bail. [36]

5. When they applied for bail, the Appellants had no notice of the extension of time granted by the Court. Moreover, the applications were made before the filing of charge sheet. Hence, the Appellants are entitled to default bail. At this stage, present Court may note here that, in the case of Sanjay Dutt as well as in the case of Bikramjit Singh , this Court held that grant of default bail does not prevent re-arrest of the Petitioners on cogent grounds after filing of charge-sheet. Thereafter, the Accused can always apply for regular bail. However, as held by this Court in the case of Mohamed Iqbal Madar Sheikh and Ors. v. State of Maharashtra, re-arrest cannot be made only on the ground of filing of charge sheet. It all depends on the facts of each case. [37]

6. Accordingly, the impugned orders passed by the Special Court granting extension to complete investigation and impugned judgment of the High Court are quashed and set aside. The Appellants shall be enlarged on default bail Under Sub-section (2) of Section 167 of Code of Criminal Procedure on conditions: (a) The Appellants shall furnish a bail bond of Rs. 2,00,000/- with appropriate sureties as may be decided by the Special Court; (b) The Appellants shall surrender their passports to the Special Court at the time of furnishing security; (c) The Appellants shall not interfere in any manner with the further investigation, if any and shall not make any effort to influence the prosecution witnesses; and (d) The Appellants shall mark regular attendance with such police station and at such periodical intervals, as may be determined by the Special Court; and (e) The Appellants shall cooperate with the Special Court for early conclusion of the trial. [38]

7. Appeals allowed. [39]

Disposition: In Favour of Accused.

• • •

Adv. Jayprakash Somani's Videos On Law

Adv. Jayprakash Somani's Videos on Law on Youtube- 'jaysomani64' channel.

1) SLP in Supreme Court / Special Leave Petitions in the Supreme Court of India

2) Transfer of Civil & Criminal Cases by the Supreme Court of India / Transfer of Matrimonial Cases

3) Appellate Jurisdiction of the Supreme Court of India

4) Jurisdictions of the Supreme Court of India

5) Public Interest Litigation in the Supreme Court of India / PIL in Supreme Court

6) Article 32 Writ Petitions in the Supreme Court of India

7) Bail Matters Top 10 Supreme Court Cases

8) FIR Quashing in High Court & Supreme Court

9) Bail & Anticipatory Bail Matters in Supreme Court

10) Insolvency & Bankruptcy Matters in the Supreme Court

11) Insolvency & Bankruptcy Code 2016 Part 1

12) Insolvency & Bankruptcy Code 2016 Part 2

13) Insolvency & Bankruptcy Code 2016 Part 3

14) Corporate Liquidation Process

15) Supreme Court Rules & Procedures Webinar of 2.5 hour on Zoom

16) RDDBFI Act, 1993 (Introduction)

17) The Indian Contact Act 1872

18) Negotiable Instruments Act (Introduction)

19) How to avoid matrimonial disputes& some more videos

20) SEBI Matters in the Supreme Court

21) Matrimonial Matters: Supreme Court's 20 Case Laws

22) Consumer Matters Supreme Court's 20 Case Laws

23) Service Matters Supreme Court's 20 Case Laws

24) How to Search Lawyer for Your Matter

25) Property Matters Supreme Court's 20 Case Laws

26) Bail Matters: Supreme Court's 20 Case Laws

27) Supreme Court / High Court Vacation Benches

28) 69000 Teacher's Recruitment Matters of UP Government in the Supreme Court

29) Contempt of Court Matters in the Supreme Court

30) Advocate Act's Matters in the Supreme Court

31) Business Law Matters in the Supreme Court

32) Banking Matters in the Supreme Court

33) Labour Law Matters in the Supreme Court

34) Arbitration Matters in the Supreme Court

35) Careers in Law -Zoom Webinar by Adv. Jayprakash Somani

36) Civil Matters in the Supreme Court

37) Consumer Protection Act | Consumer Matters in the Supreme Court

38) Corporate Matters in the Supreme Court

39) Criminal Matters in the Supreme Court

40) Role of Respondent in the Supreme Court of India

41) Motor Vehicle Accident Matters in Supreme Court with case laws

42) Article 131 Original Suits in Supreme Court

43) PIL in Supreme Court/ Public Interest Litigations in the Supreme Court of India'

44) CAB Citizenship Amendment Bill is not Unconstitutional

45) Supreme Court of India Cases & Process – Marathi

46) Legal Services Export / Export of Legal Services

47) Transfer of Matrimonial Cases by the Supreme Court of India

48) Public Interest Litigation PIL

49) The Specific Relief Act (Introduction)

50) Corporate Insolvency Resolution Process CIRP

51) ABMM's Career 5 - Careers in Law

52) Transfer of cases by Supreme Court

53) Writ Petitions in High Court & Supreme Court of India

54) Supreme Court Jurisdictions - Appeals, SLP, Writ Petitions, Transfer, Original, Review, Curative

55) LEGAL INDIA TV Show: Cases Handled in Supreme Court

56) Corporate Liquidation Process

57) Legal Services Export / Export of Legal Services

58) Corporate Laws

59) Election Matters- Supreme Court's 20 Case Laws

60) Companies Act, 2013

62) Competition Act, 2002

63) Banking Matters - Supreme Court's 20 Case Laws

64) Election Matters in the Supreme Court

65) Armed Forces Tribunal Matters in the Supreme Court

66) Compassionate Appointment Service matter

67) Foreign Exchange Management Act FEMA
68) Foreign Trade Policy 2021-26 Proposed
69) Customs Act 1962
70) Narcotic Drugs and Psychotropic Substances Act, 1985 NDPS Act
71) Foreign Trade Development & Regulation Act, 1992
72) How to Search Good Advocate in the Supreme Court of India
73) Sr. Adv Vikas Singh's Interview in Nani Palkhivala Wednesday Law Club
74) Indian Penal Code (I. P. C.)
75) Criminal Procedure Code (Cr. P. C.)
76) Commercial Courts & International Arbitration - by Mr. Jaideep Gupta, Senior Advocate in Nani Palkhivala Wednesday Law Club
77) Sr. Adv Ranji Thomos in Nani Palkhivala Wednesday Law Club
78) Urgent Matters in Supreme Court during vacations
79) 498A Bail Matters in Supreme Court
81) 376 Bail Matters in Supreme Court
82) 302, 304, 307, 308 Bail Matters in Supreme Court
83) 138, 420 Bail Matters in Supreme Court
84) POCSO Act Bail Matters in Supreme Court
85) NDPS Act Bail Matters in Supreme Court
86) What is ED (Enforcement Directorate)?
87) Prevention of Money Laundering Act, 2002 (PMLA Act)
88) Insolvency & Bankruptcy Code- Supreme Court Case Laws. Webinar in Nani Palkhivala Wednesday Law Club
89) What is NCLT & NCLAT?
90) Acquittal from 376- Supreme Court's some case laws in Nani Palkhivala Wednesday Law Club dt 28.7.22
91) Insolvency & Bankruptcy in India
92) Can we file case directly in the Supreme Court?
93) Adv. Anuja Pethia has cleared AOR Exam 2021 with 77% marks - Her interview in Nani Palkhivala Wednesday Law Club
94) Customs Act - Supreme Court Case Laws & Interview of AOR Adv. Anuja Pethia in Nani Palkhivala Law Club.
95) The Uttar Pradesh Public Service Tribunals Act, 1976
96) POCSO Act - Supreme Court Case Laws & Interview of AOR Adv. Shoumendu Mukharji & Adv. Nishant Verma in Nani Palkhivala Law Club.
97) Who Can Trigger CIRP Process Under Insolvency Law of India

98)The Uttar Pradesh Government Servant Discipline and Appeal Rules, 1999

99)CIRP Application Under Sec 7 by FC

100)Information Technology Act 2000

101)Uttar Pradesh Recruitment of Dependants of Government Servants Dying in Harness Rules, 1974

102)Foreign Exchange Management Act 1999 & Supreme Court's Case Laws on FEMA & Leading Case of AOR Exam in Nani Palkhivala Law Club.

103)Arbitration and Conciliation Act 1996 & It's Supreme Court Case Laws in Nani Palkhivala Wednesday Law Club.

104)Narcotic Drugs & Psychotropic Substances Act 1985 (NDPS Act) & It's Supreme Court Case Laws in Nani Palkhivala Wednesday Law Club.

105)Recovery of Debts and Bankruptcy Act 1993

106)Uttar Pradesh Land Revenue Code 2006

107)CIRP Application Under Sec 9 by OC

108)CIRP Application Under Sec 10 by CD

109)Hindu Succession Act, 1956

110)Maharashtra Civil Services Rules, 1981

111)Indian Contract Act, 1872 & Supreme Court's Case Laws" in Nani Palkhiwala Wednesday Law Club

112)Securities and Exchange Board of India Act, 1992 i. e. SEBI Act 1992 & Case Laws on Insiders Trading" in Nani Palkhiwala Wednesday Law Club

113)Moratorium Under Section 14 of IBC, 2016

114)Hindu Marriage Act, 1955

115)Maharashtra Land Revenue Code, 1966

116)64 Leading Cases of AOR Exam Session 1 :- Cases 1 to16 in Nani Palkhiwala Wednesday Law Club

117)64 Leading Cases of AOR Exam Session 2: Cases 17 to 32 in Nani Palkhivala Wednesday Law Club

118)64 Leading Cases of AOR Examination Session 3: Cases 33 to 48 in Nani Palkhivala Wednesday Law Club

119)64 Leading Cases of AOR Exam Session 4: Cases 49 to 64 in Nani Palkhivala Wednesday Law Club

120) Labour Laws of India: Part 1 - 4 New Labour Law Codes of India

121) New Labour Laws Part 2 The Code on Wages, 2019

122) New Labour Laws Part 3:- The Code on Social Security, 2020

123) Argue in English Fluently & Confidently - Two months online course.

124) SLP Admission in the Supreme Court. 2023 (Hindi)

125) Transfer of Petitions from the Supreme Court (Hindi)

126) Review Petition in the Supreme Court.(Hindi)

127) Recovery of debts from the Company (Hindi)

128) How to scarch 'Good Insolvency & Bankruptcy Consultant?' (HINDI)

129) Curative Petition in the Supreme Court

130) AFT Appeals in the Supreme Court (HINDI)

131) NCLAT's Appeals in the Supreme Court.

132) Transfer Petition: Which matters can we transfer?

133) SLP Types of SLP in the Supreme court of India (English).

134) Argue in English Fluently and Confidently in the High Court & Supreme Court'.

• • •

List Of Adv. Jayprakash Somani's Published Books

1. Supreme Court of India's Leading Case Laws on 'Insolvency & Bankruptcy Code 2016'
2. Bail Matters – Supreme Court's Latest Leading Case Laws
3. Arbitration Matters- Supreme Court's Latest Leading Case Laws
4. Property Matters - Supreme Court's Latest Leading Case Laws
5. Matrimonial Matters- Supreme Court's Latest Leading Case Laws
6. Election Matters- Supreme Court's Latest Leading Case Laws
7. SEBI Matters- Supreme Court's Latest Leading Case Laws
8. Banking Matters- Supreme Court's Latest Leading Case Laws
9. Service Matters- Supreme Court's Latest Leading Case Laws
10. Contempt of Court Matters- Supreme Court's Latest Leading Case Laws
11. Consumer Protection Matters- Supreme Court's Latest Leading Case Laws
12. Corporate Law- Supreme Court's Latest Leading Case Laws
13. Supreme Court's AOR Exam- Leading Cases
14. Armed Force Tribunal - Supreme Court's Latest Leading Case Laws
15. Acquittal From 376 - Supreme Court's Latest Leading Case Laws
16. Negotiable instrument – Supreme Court's Latest Leading Case Laws
17. Contract Act- Supreme Court's Latest Leading Case Laws
18. Insider trading- Supreme Court's Latest Leading Case Laws
19. Foreign Exchange and Management Act- Supreme Court's Latest Leading Case Laws
20. Income Tax Act- Supreme Court's Latest Leading Case Laws
21. Company Law- Supreme Court's Latest Leading Case Laws
22. Competition & Monopoly Matters- Supreme Court's Latest Leading Case Laws
23. Compassionate Appointment- Service Matters- Supreme Court's Latest Leading Case Laws
24. Compulsory Retirement- Service Matters- Supreme Court's Latest Leading Case Laws
25. Voluntary Retirement- Service Matters- Supreme Court's Latest Leading Case Laws
26. Removal/Dismissal/Termination from Service- Supreme Court's Latest Leading Case Laws

27. Seniority- Service Matter- Supreme Court's Latest Leading Case Laws
28. Promotion- Service Matter- Supreme Court's Latest Leading Case Laws
29. Equal Pay for Equal Work- Service Matter- Supreme Court's Latest Leading Case Laws
30. Condition of Service- Service Matter- Supreme Court's Latest Leading Case Laws
31. Customs Act- Supreme Court's Leading Case Laws
32. Information Technology Act- Supreme Court's Leading Case Laws
33. SEC. 125 CR. P. C.- Supreme Court's Leading Case Laws
34. SEC. 498A OF I. P. C.- Supreme Court's Leading Case Laws
35. MOTOR VEHICLE ACT- Supreme Court's Leading Case Laws
36. CONDITION OF SERVICE- SERVICE MATTER- Supreme Court's Leading Case Laws
37. SUSPENSION- SERVICE MATTER- Supreme Court's Leading Case Laws
38. Reservation in SC, ST, OBC- Service Matter- Supreme Court's Leading Case Laws
39. NARCOTIC DRUGS AND PSYCHOTROPIC SUBSTANCES (NDPS) ACT - Supreme Court of India's Latest Leading Case Laws
40. SEC 302 IPC - Supreme Court of India's Latest Leading Case Laws
41. PROTECTION OF CHILDREN FROM SEXUAL OFFENCES ACT (POCSO) - Supreme Court of India's Latest Leading Case Laws
42. PMLA ACT BAIL MATTERS - Supreme Court of India's Leading Case Laws
43. SEC 376 BAIL MATTERS - Supreme Court of India's Leading Case Laws
44. SEC 302 BAIL MATTERS - Supreme Court of India's Leading Case Laws
45. POCSO ACT BAIL MATTERS - Supreme Court of India's Leading Case Laws
46. JUVENILE JUSTICE ACT- Supreme Court of India's Leading Case Laws
47. TRANSFER OF PROPERTY ACT- Supreme Court of India's Leading Case Laws
48. PROFESSIONAL ETHICS OF ADVOCATES- AOR EXAM- SUPREME COURT'S LEADING CASE LAWS
49. WHITE COLLAR CRIME- SUPREME COURT'S LEADING CASE LAWS
50. SEC 302 BAIL MATTERS- SUPREME COURT'S LEADING CASE LAWS
51. SEC 7 IBC 2016 - SUPREME COURT'S LATEST LEADING CASE LAW
52. ADVERSE POSSESSION IN PROPERTY MATTER - SUPREME COURT'S LATEST LEADING CASE LAWS
53. FOOD SAFETY AND STANDARD ACT 2006' - SUPREME COURT AND

HIGH COURT's LEADING CASE LAWS

54. ARMED FORCE TRIBUNAL ACT- SUPREME COURT'S LATEST LEADING CASE LAWS

55. ESSENTIAL COMMODITIES ACT 1955- SUPREME COURT'S LATEST LEADING CASE LAWS

56. FOREIGN TRADE DEVELOPMENT AND REGULATION ACT'- SUPREME COURT AND HIGH COURT'S LEADING CASE LAWS

57. PARTNERSHIP ACT 1932- SUPREME COURT'S LEADING CASE LAWS

58. COTPA ACT 2003 - SUPREME COURT AND HIGH COURT'S LEADING CASE LAWS

59. DOMESTIC VIOLENCE ACT 2005 - SUPREME COURT'S LEADING CASE LAWS

60. DOWRY PROHIBITION ACT 1961 - SUPREME COURT'S LATEST CASE LAWS

61. SUPREME COURT'S AOR EXAM- DRAFTING Formates of more than 25 Drafts for AOR Exam Paper 2 - Drafting

62. SPECIFIC RELIEF ACT 1963- SUPREME COURT'S LATEST LEADING CASE LAWS

63. PREVENTION OF MONEY LAUNDERING ACT 2002- SUPREME COURT'S LATEST CASE LAWS

64. PREVENTION OF CORRUPTION ACT 1988- SUPREME COURT'S LATEST CASE LAWS

65. PREVENTION OF ILLICIT TRAFFIC OF NDPS ACT 1988- SUPREME COURT'S LATEST CASE LAWS

Books are available online in India
1. Notion Press: https://notionpress.com/author/jayprakash_somani
2. Amazon: https://www.amazon.in/s?k=jayprakash+somani
3. Flipkart: https://www.flipkart.com/search?q=Jayprakash%20Somani

Books are available online at International Market
4. Amazon International: https://www.amazon.com/s?k=jayprakash+somani
5. Amazon United Kingdom: https://www.amazon.co.uk/s?k=jayprakash+somani
6. E-Books/Kindle edition at National & International Level: https://www.amazon.in/s?k=jaypraksh+somani

• • •

Adv Jayprakash Somani's Online Legal & Import Export Courses

Download our app to get access to our Free Videos, Free Bare Acts, Free Study Material in Legal as well as International Business Regime.

Android App Link ;-https://clpandrea.page.link/cmSm

Ios APp Link :-https://apps.apple.com/us/app/classplus/id1324522260

Login with org code ;- (qywzji)

Web Link ;-https://qywzji.courses.store/

Download App on Google play store - Type

Jayprakash Somani SupremeCourt

Legal Courses :

1. **SLP- Bail Matters- Drafting & Successful Arguing in the Supreme Court.**
2. **SLP- Succession Matters- Drafting & Successful Arguing in the Supreme Court.**
3. **Legal Vocabulary & its practice pattern to Argue in High Court and**

Supreme Court / Improve Your Legal English.
4. SLP- Property Matters - Drafting and Successful Arguing in the Supreme Court.

International Business Courses -

1. Agri Products Exports - Scope from India.
2. Textile Exports - Scope from India.
3. Export Import Procedure -Perfect Documentation & It's Management.
4. Jewellery Exports -Scope from India.
5. Export Import Finance Management with LC, ECGC & Venture Capital.
6. Shipping & Logistics in International Business with live links of Ports, ICDs, CHAs etc.
7. International Business Marketing Part 1: Finding Potential & Genuine Buyers for Exports and Suppliers for Imports.
8. International Business Marketing Part 2: Communication Skill to take repeated orders from Potential Buyers.

•••